HOUSE
OF SPIRITS

HOUSE
OF SPIRITS

A story of souls Based upon the true stories from
301 Wickersham & The Pastor of Howard County

J.S. BUTCHER

XULON PRESS

Xulon Press
2301 Lucien Way #415
Maitland, FL 32751
407.339.4217
www.xulonpress.com

Paperback ISBN-13: 978-1-6628-3858-3
Hard Cover ISBN-13: 978-1-6628-3859-0
Ebook ISBN-13: 978-1-6628-3860-6

ACKNOWLEDGEMENTS

I would like to recognize my mother and Christy and Gary Ripperger for their encouragement and financial backing to take these stories to the reader. I would also like to thank professor at Ozark Christian College, pastor at Park Plaza Christian Church in Joplin, Missouri, and personal friend, Mark Scott for devoting his lunch hours to guide me and encourage me in this endeavor. Countless hours of editing went into this project, so I thank my anonymous editor for working through chronic headaches. Any remaining errors in the text can be attributed to me rather than him. Finally I would like to acknowledge The Pastor of Howard County who is never referred to by name for reasons that will become obvious. Thank you to each person who has picked up the inspired 'Word of God' and made it come alive in the lives of others; you are the unseen heroes of the earth – you and your stories will be remembered, and some of them will now be told.

Prologue

FATE & VIRTUE

The Pastor's study was comprised of three things: wood, leather, and paper – lots of paper. Red mahogany library panels lined the walls which supported multiple rows of bookshelves. *Books*. Books were The Pastor's wallpaper. Books were the tools of his trade. Every pastoral topic was there – world religions, divorce recovery, martyrdom of the faith, but the book that lay open on his desk was ***THE GREAT PANDEMIC OF 21ST CENTURY AMERICA – THE HOMELESS***. There were other books on the shelves as well; favorite books intended for recreational reading such as the writings of J.R.R. Tolkien. It was the epic struggle of good vs. evil that caught his fancy, where the fate of a few found virtue.

Darkness had arrived in Howard County and the only two table lamps in the study tried in vain to chase away the stubborn shadows. The deep red mahogany of the library walls and the dark hardwood floor ate what light entered the room. The 'blackjack' oak logs in the open hearth gave off a scent of hot cinnamon as the fire spit and popped, sending out sparks of red and gold. The Pastor watched the flames as if in a trance, his mind given over to the open book on his desk.

The Pastor had earlier spent hours in a vacant parking lot just a few blocks from the local homeless shelter sitting in the privacy of his old rusty pickup truck. A shiny thermos stood next to him, a stark contrast to his dilapidated ride. Both the truck and thermos had their fair share of dents and dings, but the thermos could be replaced. The truck however could not. It was a gift from his late father, so the truck would remain. He sat and watched as the nightly shelter occupants were turned out each morning to walk the city streets during the day. Whether in the blistering August heat, the April showers of Spring or the wind driven snows of a biting January, they walked in a never ending circuit of unrest until darkness once again claimed the land and allowed them entrance to their only haven in life – the shelter. It was an endless journey through the wilderness of despair.

It occurred to The Pastor that the Hebrew children of God had wandered for forty years through the desert sands in their pilgrimage to the promised land. None who initially took the journey made it to its completion – but their children did.

"The children of the homeless people must be spared from this", thought The Pastor to himself as the whispering sounds of the study echoed in his ears.

The ambience of the room and the heady topic of the night caused him to imagine that Gandalf himself was coming for a night meeting. But It wasn't Gandalf he was expecting, it was Wayne – the chairperson for the Church of Christ financial committee. It was the intention of The Pastor to convince Wayne that the Church needed to purchase the house at 301 Wickersham as a halfway house for the needy and the homeless.

'The Pastor of Howard County' sat at his desk and stared into the fire and took in the scene before him as he fiddled with the 'Newton's cradle' in the center of his desk. The shiny silver balls reflected the red - orange flames of the logs as they softly clanged together in a hypnotic cadence, his mind ever on the book before him – 'THE GREAT PANDEMIC. The Pastor's wife had given him the cradle. She died young and her husband's heart was buried with her, taking any hope the man had for children as well. So, the Church became his wife; and his flock became his children.

Wickersham ran perpendicular to Main Street where The Church of Christ sat and the house at 301 Wickersham was barely a sidewalk's distance from the Church's parking lot. The house was in pretty good shape for its age. The white wood siding had just been painted for an open house that the owners hoped would result in a quick sale. It had new shingles and the front porch boasted of a huge picture window and a front entry door that reminded the Pastor of a hobbit door made of glass. *"It would be a perfect place for the Church to nurture and care for families in need of a fresh start in life"*, he thought to himself. "The 'pairs and spares' Sunday School class could meet there until the right family comes along...". As fate would have it, it would not be all that long. The fate of a few had an appointment with the virtue of The Pastor and none of them would ever be the same.

Headlights from Wayne's old Chevrolet Bel Air car arced across the ceiling and walls of The Pastor's study announcing the chairperson's arrival and temporarily chasing the cobwebs from The Pastor's thoughts. Wayne loved that old car. The 1957 was in mint condition; restored from years of abuse and mistreatment, just like Wayne. It was a turquoise convertible with white fins that looked like a shark out of water. In the summer, Wayne would take the family for ice cream and cruise down Main Street with the top down. Wayne would wear a lopsided grin as he licked on his cone and drove down the street with one hand on the steering wheel while his other hand held his treat in a death grip for fear the wind would steal it away. The top remained up on that night though with the outside temperatures in the lower thirties and a weather forecast that warned of heavy snows by morning.

Wayne was a big man in his sixties. He had rough hands that belonged to a lifelong farmer and a very big heart which was on its last leg of Wayne's life. He was the second generation son of a farmer, so his family wasn't new to the corn fields of central Indiana. His old heart was too old to farm, but it wasn't too weak to embrace his role in the Church. Wayne was only twelve years old when his parents were killed in a farming accident. Wayne Senior got his arm wrapped around their combine auger: his wife came to Wayne Senior's rescue only to get her whole self in there with him. It doesn't take too long to bleed out in a John Deere combine – but they died together. Wayne Junior was left as an orphan and no one to take him in. A neighbor allowed the boy to stay in a hired hand shack on the back of their property. Little Wayne put himself through school and held down a job at a local diner as a plate washer. That's what kept him fed and the little man survived. That's why Wayne agreed that night to The Pastor's wild and ambitious plan for the church to come to the aid of the homeless. If there was anyone in Howard County who could empathize with the needs and hazards found in life it was the big rough farmer.

It was strange that a meeting which would come to affect so many people in so many different ways would end so quickly, but Wayne's grandson was point guard for the Kokomo WildKats and they were taking on Newcastle that Friday night. Wayne wanted to be there for the tip off. That kid was Wayne's delight, so when the pastor noticed the big man check his cheap Timex wrist watch for the third time, the men parted company. The lamps were turned off in the study and The Pastor of Howard County moved off to the kitchen. There at the table which sat in front of his patio doors, with a cup of hot decaf in hand, and in the peaceful background night - light from the cooking stove, the pastor watched the snow as it began to fall. *Fate had indeed been set in motion …*

TABLE OF CONTENTS

...IF THESE WALLS COULD TALK

Cottonwood was caught up in a summer wind and blew above the tall grasses that swayed in the warm breeze. Yellow and black bumblebees took turns as they moved from daisies, once planted with care, and untended wild flowers gone to seed. The unkempt yard had a life of its own which added a punctuation mark to the truth that the rundown house standing sentry over the scene had been abandoned by the people who once lived there. Only the insects remained. So, the old, deserted building watched – and remembered.

The house would have been demolished long ago had it not sat on land owned by the Church of Christ. The Church itself had been abandoned for just as long as the parsonage (at least that was what the people called it) but the Howard County Council for the preservation of Historical Sites had value for the old church. The parsonage however was on its own. It was just as well, ever since The Pastor had died the town had lost the heart to go there.

The wood grain of the gray weathered siding of the parsonage looked like coarse channels in a parched dry riverbed, flowing toward the front doorbell, forming a knot that resembled an open mouth screaming for moisture that never came. A massive picture window overlooked most of the front porch. Eventually the glass had cracked in a million shattered pieces but had held together by some inexplicable spell. There had been no one there to enjoy those Hoosier sunsets anymore, but when the broken pieces of glass caught the final rays of the setting sun, it was like the Fourth of July inside that old house. Rainbows of color would march across the walls and disappear in the ceiling. It was an endless loop on the reel of time but only the old, abandoned house could see the show.

The Pastor was gone, as was 'donut Sunday' and the candy that the kids would pass out; the children's sermon; all were gone. Times had changed and some things were just lost. Millennials hadn't aspired to live in the country or in a house like the old 'parsonage' with plenty of land and a white picket fence or raise children with dirt on their faces from playing in the nearby field. Even marriage itself was left behind as an old relic of claustrophobic values. Youths moved into town and took up residence with whomever they chose, in housing complexes offering free internet for their gadgets and their movies. Nor did people shop like they once had, they shopped on- line and had packages delivered to their door. The local miniature golf course had closed, along with the 18-hole course across from the town park. Young people had preferred electronic golf, and electronic batting cages. Who wanted to sweat in the heat of a bright summer sun or risk a rain - out at the ball field when you can golf the course of your choice in air conditioning or play baseball at your favorite baseball field. Electronic versions of Wrigley Field and Comisky Park had replaced real life. So, the parsonage and the old Church were given over to chapters of history. Millennials did not hold much value for history, so no one remembered the sermons - or the lessons - or the history.

The walls inside the old parsonage had seen things however; heard things. Memories had been etched into those walls like a sharp chisel applied to soft stone. The markings on those walls had become permanent, and the walls were ready to talk. There were stories to be told.

stories like these.

Chapter One

THE GENEROUS THIEF

The father of The Pastor of Howard County had held on to life as if by a silver thread. He had begun smoking at the young age of twelve. Just where he procured those first cigarettes he no longer remembered; just that he and his brother (Little Chum) hunkered down behind the family outhouse, away from the prying eyes of his father, and thereby writing on the slate of his own life how he would eventually end his years.

The gold in his life now wasn't life itself, but the phone calls from his two boys reaching out frequently for fatherly advice. One boy had moved to the distant Ozarks and chose the life of a business man while the second son entered the ministry and spent the years of his own life serving others. The gruff old father was fully qualified to dole out morsels of counsel in either situation since his own life had involved both enterprises – business and ministry.

"Everything in life comes with a price son, nothing in life is free. There is a price to be paid for doing nothing and there is a price that you will have to pay for getting involved. Everything exacts a price. Also, if you do choose to get involved, there will be a payday someday. But, just like the thirty pieces of silver, you may not always like the payment."

The Gospel According to Matthew… chapter 25: vv. 34-36

"THE LEAST OF THESE"…

Silence can be an effective tool in preaching. Silence can be used to drive home an important point. Silence can be used to make the audience uncomfortable so the speaker can drive home a meaning of great significance. The silence which hung in the sanctuary on this fateful Sunday morning however was unintended. The bright morning sun reflected off the snow that had fallen the evening before and lit up the stained – glass windows like neon lights that splayed across the sanctuary walls and took The Pastor back to his study and the open book on his desk. Visions of the homeless played in his mind's eye, as well. He saw them with worn out shoes that no one would want and tattered jeans that had both seen too many summers.

But the Pastor of Howard County came out of his reverie and looked out upon his flock and saw the concern for him on their faces. So, he ended his unintended silence and made his case for why it was a good idea to purchase the property located behind the church. "The world in which we live today has seen great change. People wear masks – not to hide their face but to stay alive. We have seen a pandemic or two in this country and we may see more. There is one pandemic that simply will not go away however - the homeless." The Pastor presented his arguments and the people listened.

The Holy Spirit moved through the crowd in the sanctuary that morning, touching one person and then moving on to another. A young boy sitting in the fourth row from the front thought how he could donate his earnings from his newspaper route to the cause while a little girl daydreamed of how she could decorate one of the bedrooms of the house on Wickersham with her dolls and her favorite quilt that her own grandmother had made for her bed. Wayne sat there and wondered what his own childhood would have been like if something like this had been available. A lone tear sought passage down his cheek; alone just like the little boy left behind by two loving parents. By the time Jane sat down to play the benediction the audience was in a trance. Everyone pondered the deep and impactful question outlined by The Pastor: *"Darkness is a very real and tangible thing; it can be seen on the corner in front of the neighborhood market. It's in the classroom of your school and you pass it on the street as you venture home from a hard day's work. Darkness has a life of its own and it seeks, ever* *virulent – it seeks. What are you willing to do to beat it back, even for the briefest of moments. What will **you** do?"*

One lone soul sat on the back row of the upper balcony. She had slipped in unawares to the greeters after the song service had concluded. Granny's mind was in two places at the same time – The Pastor's sermon (and the personal hope she found there) and the most hated place she knew on planet Earth – extreme Eastern Kentucky. She had been called *'Granny'* for as long as she could remember. Her shiny chrome spectacles sat on the end of an upturned, sun kissed nose, and her gray hair was pulled back so tight that it virtually made her eyes squint. Every resemblance to Granny of the Beverly Hillbillies was so evident that even the most cursory of assessments of her confirmed it. There was no way of remembering who first referred to her as such, it was so long ago, but the name stuck.

Granny grew up in the eastern most part of Kentucky. Only a rutted out dirt road separated her little town from West Virginia and the coal mines where the villagers went to work, and often to die. It seemed as if her entire life was overgrown with weeds and tall trees that blocked out the sun by day and the moon by night. People went missing in that part of the country, never to be found again. It was a dangerous place to be and be from. She went to school there (if one could call it school), she married there and had children there - the back woods of eastern Kentucky.

The family down the dirt road from her trailer had all the earmarks of worldly success – a billiard table in the front lawn and two red velvet recliners on the front

porch next to the wood pile. Granny never did under-
stand how the chairs weren't always soaked from rain and
morning dew – the wood pile certainly was. Church was
different there too – not like this one she had wandered
into by chance.

One good road led into her little town and the same
road led out. The county couldn't afford to give the
place a respectable paved Main Street, and certainly not
concrete. Every so often the highway department would
show up and spray that road with hot oil and cover it
with limestone chips. Cars and foot traffic had to pound
the chips into the hot oil. The county couldn't afford a
steam – powered roller. All in all, it made a pretty good
road. It wasn't so great for the shoes, however.

The first (and last) building that met a traveler coming
into town was the old town church. Granny had always
thought the place was so old it must have been built by
Daniel Boone himself. It was an old log and stone structure
held together by the same grit that the townspeople
possessed. On the very top of the old structure was a
new steeple, shiny white with a giant silver cross on the
top. When the mid – afternoon sun hit that cross, it could
be seen by half the county. It was the only thing that was
new in those parts for miles, but the people there wanted
to make a statement somewhere and they chose the local
church to do it. "When someone comes into this town we
want them to know we mean business about our religion
and our Bibles!".; the former Mayor had said in a speech
during a 'Veteran's Day in the park' celebration.

While the outside of the old church reflected the hopes and determination of a ragged tenacious people, the inside reflected their personalities. The pews were cut from local maple trees and milled at a nearby saw mill, polished to a sheen. The gashes and gouges in the wood conveyed stories of their own, of revivals and exuberant prayer meetings and long Sunday services. The little town didn't possess a theatre or anything resembling a shopping center. Church was the focal point of civic activity.

Sunday morning services were fairly normal for that time and place. Songs were sung out of old song books that were neatly tucked into the book racks on the backs of each pew. Men and boys wore old suits with white starched shirts and skinny black ties while the women all arrived in the best dresses that their budgets could afford. It was the evening services, however, where things got interesting. The men left their jackets and ties at home and in exchange brought the most awful creatures Granny could imagine – snakes! There were copperheads, water moccasins and rattlers. The more dangerous and venomous the better. After the sermon, the snake handlers would take the stage – men drenched with evening sweat in a hot and stuffy building. The fluorescent lights would flicker and pop, adding to the surreal mood. Men and an occasional bold woman would hold up a snake above their head, calling attention to the scene. Little boys watched in amazement and little girls covered their mouths while most mothers cringed with undisguised revulsion. Granny didn't always go to Sunday evening services. Her life had enough scary circumstances. She didn't need to add to her own raw emotional state.

Granny left room for the beliefs of others. Her own brother was said to have a special 'spiritual gift' that the preacher called a 'Burn Reliever'. People would come from counties all around with bad burns and have James Easton lay hands on the damaged skin. It was the most incredible thing Granny had ever witnessed. One minute someone would be in such great pain, and nearly come unglued when James laid hands on the burn, but within seconds the pain was gone. When her brother took his hands away, there wasn't even a red mark where the burn had been.

So, Granny sat this day in the farthest corner of the back row of the balcony of the little church in Howard County Indiana listening as the hope from The Pastor's message played at the corners of her imagination. "What would this crazy hopeful idea do for me if I was the first person to live at 301 Wickersham that The Pastor is talking about?" And she reminisced about the passage of time and the events that landed her in that distant church clinging to this new hope and urgent need. Her mind was still in two places at the same time.

Granny figured that no one gets up in the morning and intentionally messes up their lives and certainly she did not intend to either. She had dated a local boy, married too young and had two little girls too early. Frank, her husband, had told her when they were just dating: "I'm going to get out of this crummy little town and shake the dust off my boots. I'm not going to work coal in an underground grave and die a young man from breathing in the dust off the Appalachian Mountains!" Granny had mistakenly assumed that Frank was going to take her out of *'that crummy little town'* with him but he didn't. Frank got out of town all right as a truck driver for an over the road hauler. He got out of town and saw what the rest of the country had to offer and how other people lived, and what they owned and ate, and what they did for recreation. Frank was always glad to get back on the road and leave the Appalachian foothills in his rearview mirror. He never looked back but he reluctantly returned home. He had to. Frank had a wife and two little girls, but he resented it with every fiber of his being.

It was obvious to anyone who knew Frank that the man had spent his whole life leaving things behind. Frank's father was a lifelong coal miner in the depths of the nearby mountains. His dad left every morning with his lunch box and thermos for a day of digging up black diamonds only to return home each night worn and beaten – until one day he didn't. Bodies were recovered from the mine shaft cave – in, but the spirit of little Frank never was. He left it behind in a sodden dreary mist at a grave side ceremony on the day when he left his dad behind.

Frank quit going to school and left the books and reading and hope for a brighter future for himself behind as well, in an effort to help his mother make financial ends meet at home. He took any job he could find. Little Frank swept up hair at the only barber shop in town and cleaned dishes at the only diner that was there. Frank had left a lot of things behind in his life, except his hatred for that 'crummy little town'. He kept that in the top pocket of his bib overalls like an old black and white photo of some-thing valuable. If any fond or precious memory would surface in his heart or mind, Frank would pull out the old emotional and tattered black and white photo of hatred for his situation and push back anything positive trying to surface.

Every Saturday evening Frank would leave the place he hated most and left a few more marks on the person he resented most – Granny. It was a no lose situation for Frank. He headed out to see the world and take out his frustrations before he left for the week. But every Sunday morning Granny would show up at Church with a new set of bruises or cuts. Most of the town that knew Frank nursed a low opinion of the man.

Frank was fascinated by the cargo he carried on his eighteen – wheeler. He absolutely adored the Queen Anne furniture he picked up from the Amish furniture factory. The ornate moldings and hand carved ornamentation were fascinating to him. Frank was determined to have that furniture with all its glory in every room of his home someday. Once each month he would travel the two lane highway 446 into Bloomington, Indiana and drop off a load of Amish made furniture at the Showers Factory for distribution. Willard Godsey, foreman at the factory, was always there to greet Frank with a warm handshake and a hot cup of coffee. And on his way out of town, Frank would pass the Showers Mansion on Walnut street just three blocks from the factory. It was a magnificent red brick palace with lead paned windows and an intricate cobblestone sidewalk. The mere sight of the grand structure added more fuel to Frank's ambitions.

On other trips to the Hoosier state, he would haul Kentucky made maple syrup to the Burns Wholesale Grocery, also in Bloomington. One day Frank ventured into the front office to get signatures on his bill of lading and saw on the old oak desk the family photos there. Two teenaged girls stood in front of a black vintage sedan with one foot on the running board, a wizened mother stood at a distance. "A modern version of 'Bonnie and Claudette'," thought Frank. All three had a snicker about a secret only they knew, and which the photo would not reveal. On the opposite side of the desk stood another photo of a girl in French braids and a tasseled cow skin jacket that had long hanging fringe. She was hugging a patchwork pony. In the corner of the photo in the longhand script that clearly belonged to Roy Burns, the owner, was the phrase – *'The Princess & The Duchess'*. As he left the office, Frank reached for the old warehouse office door to close it behind him and noticed a third picture fastened securely to the back of the door. Frank opened the door just enough to study the painting.He recognized it from Sunday School, when he used to attend as a boy. It was the Messiah, Jesus, the Son of God who stood before a closed door and knocked. Frank was told that the door had no handle from the outside because – *"you have to open the door to let the Savior in"*. Roy clearly had his treasures in life, but it wasn't appealing to the ambitious truck driver, so Frank turned and walked from the office through the darkened warehouse to his waiting truck and left just one more thing behind – any hope of his reclamation.

Frank dropped crates of syrup off at restaurants and grocery stores alike all along Indiana highway 446, through towns like Gnawbone and Stoney Lonesome. On one occasion Frank met up with one of Roy Burns' outside salesmen – a lean quirky guy with a lopsided smile, black wavy hair and flaming red socks. The man seemed absolutely enamored with life and Frank wondered why anyone would be that happy just being an order taker.

It was the third rotation of shipments that really caused Frank (and Granny) trouble – Kentucky bourbon. Pallets of charred oak barrels housed gallons upon gallons of bourbon and took up half of the semi while other pallets of stacked cases of glass bottles of the aged stuff took up the other half of the truck. Frank had a system on how to short the invoices and charge them off as "damaged in freight" and "destroyed at the delivery site" in exchange for free goods from the various restaurants who would play the game. It wasn't difficult to imagine how glass bottles could get broken in transit on those narrow two lane Hoosier highways with potholes, so Frank never did get caught. He was living in tall cotton those weeks. His fraud profits while on the road allowed him to enjoy the finest cuts of prime rib and filet mignon and Kentucky's best to wash it down. Frank particularly enjoyed those weeks and imbibed joyfully and heavily upon the fruits of his sordid labors all the way home. The home boys grew cheap moonshine, and the law looked the other way, but Frank drank the best straight from the glass bottles they were shipped in.

It was the season of change. The oppressive temperatures of the previous three months had given way to the cooling of Autumn. The red hot heat of summer had been gathered up it seemed and deposited into the leaves of orange on the Maples and flaming reds of the Sumac. Granny took it all in as she walked the chip and seal pavement of Main Street on her way to the Church that 'Daniel Boone had built'. She walked with a limp that day. Frank had been particularly mean to her before he had departed on another 'Kentucky bourbon run'.

Granny was up against a block wall, and she knew it. Something would have to change. She wasn't the only person in human history to be at a seeming dead end in life, it had happened to multitudes over the centuries. It had happened to Moses and the slaves of Egypt with a mighty body of water in their face and a raging army at their backs whose only mission in their lives was to take theirs. It couldn't have been easy for Moses but at least he had spoken with God on the mountain top when He had appeared in a burning bush. All the Hebrews knew were the mud pits of their captors and the cruel sting of their whips. *"Faith and trust –* that's what's needed," thought Granny.

It had happened in the days of King Hezekiah as well. Common people just like Granny hunkered down behind the barricaded walls of The Temple of God in Jerusalem while the Assyrian army waited to kill them all. No one inside the gates needed to be told just what would happen to them if the army breached the walls, it was perfectly clear to everyone. The Assyrians were well known for taking what did not belong to them and doing unspeakable things to those from whom they were taken. But King Hezekiah did what Granny knew needed to be done – lay out her case before the God of the angel armies

"THE ENEMY AT THE GATES".
(Isaiah 36 – 37)

It was the week's sermon topic; posted on the church sign out front. It was the custom of that preacher to post his topic so the townspeople could meditate and pray about the message of the week. If anyone had an enemy at the gates it was Granny. The situation with Frank had become unbearable – and unsafe.

*"Dear God, I need your help more now than at any time in my life. I so desperately need out of my husband's cruel hands. You made Earth in just six days; Frank will be home again in the same amount of time. Can you make **me** a new Earth? Will you come to my aid?"*

"Be careful what you ask for child." Granny heard the voice of her mother speak to her from her

childhood. "God can always help His children, but the passage may not be as easy as you think."

Granny pushed through the heavy double doors that led into the church sanctuary with great effort that day. She hobbled down the center aisle and took her usual seat as conversations stopped and congregants watched the old girl with the busted lip and swollen face. Granny wasn't embarrassed anymore by the stares; it was just part of life; at least life with Frank.

The Preacher was predictable. His sermons always consisted of four main points and the message never lasted more than forty minutes. Once the song service concluded the old man straightened up his tall lanky frame and took his usual place behind the familiar pulpit and looked out over his people. Faces from the left side of the sanctuary made eye contact with the preacher and they cautiously directed his gaze over to Granny. He was well acquainted with the sight of personal damage and despair and Granny wore both that day like a heavy black cloak, soiled with the years of abuse that had been placed upon her.

The man laid out his main points to the congregation and they dutifully listened:

I. SPREAD OUT THE LETTER. Hezekiah received a blasphemous letter from the Assyrians and the King of Judah laid the letter before the Lord.

II. <u>WORSHIP</u>. God knows who He is. God needs to know that *you* know who He is.
III. <u>MAKE YOUR REQUEST</u>. "Just ask".
IV. <u>GOD ALMIGHTY IS HIS NAME – HE IS YOUR CHAMPION</u>. He parted the Red Sea, He killed giants, He made the Earth is six days. He is fully capable of making you a new Earth in six days.

"Behold; the enemy is at the gates. His spears are raised to the heavens and the sun glints off them in numbers too many to count. They stand at the ready in their armor and shields ready to devour a helpless people, but the God of the angel armies breathes on them, and they disappear like dried leaves before a raging fire. God's people have always been up against a dead end, but it's just an allusion – to test your faith...". The preacher's sermon was good, and it gave Granny hope.

"Dear Father, you killed 185,000 enemies of God in just one night, I know you can help me." Granny prayed for help from the One who destroys armies. It occurred to her that just one of God's angels had killed 185,000 Assyrians in just one night – "roughly the speed of light". Granny remembered the words from the sermon as she walked home. She continued to seek the help of the God of the angel armies in her plight with Frank.

"Be careful what you ask for child." Granny heard the voice of her mother speak to her from her childhood once again. "God can always help His children, but the passage may not be as easy as you think."

"It's too late to be cautious mom, I simply cannot do this anymore. It's time for a change." Granny meditated on the memory of her mother and the words of the Preacher.

There was a lot to think about that afternoon as Granny sat in her trailer. The sliding glass door that led to the vegetable garden stood open and she sat with her 12 gauge shotgun protecting the last of her harvest from the coyotes. Frank never left money behind for groceries, so she planted a garden. Other household items were needed too, so she bartered out her services to the working mothers in the town, watching ng their children in exchange for eggs, meat, and sundries. As a result, everyone in the community knew Granny and loved her dearly. Most everyone knew what she was up against. The linen curtains on the sides of the sliding glass door rustled in the Autumn breeze. Yes, change was in the air.

It was the end of a particularly profitable 'Kentucky bourbon run' to southern Indiana and Frank sat in a diner in French Lick nursing the last drop of a last cup of coffee, along with his old grudge against Granny. "I was duped into marrying that girl', thought Frank. "She bewitched me with her innocence and backward ways. I need to make some changes and just as soon as I get home, I will make them." Yes, the winds of change were in the air for Frank too.

It was late when the headlights of Frank's semi turned down the lane to the hated hometown trailer. The long trip home had given him plenty of time to dig into the crates of the procured bourbon. By the time he got home he was heavily under the influence of the demon in the bottle. Frank was a 'mean drunk' and when he walked into the bedroom and saw Granny sleeping there he stubbed out his cigarette on the back of his wife's neck. *"Why did you do that"*, Granny sobbed and lurched to the ice box in the kitchen for ice to place on the wound. "Because they ain't no ashtray," Frank drooled.

The mean truck driver had momentum by then and took out a knife from one of the kitchen drawers and told Granny 'he was going to cut her into fine little pieces and feed them to the snakes at the church'. Granny cautiously retraced her steps to the patio door where she kept her shotgun. As Frank leaned in to drive the knife home, Granny pulled the trigger. Half of Frank's face was instantly gone. His agony was intense by the time the Sheriff arrived.

"You need to leave Granny. Take some clothes and Frank's wallet and checkbook and leave – quickly", the Sheriff instructed. She hastily put one small bag on the seat next to her in the family's pickup and left her trailer, her church, and her life. In the truck's rearview mirror she could see two distinct flashes of light and she could feel the faint but unmistakable percussion of her 12 gauge shotgun as the Sheriff finished what Granny had begun with Frank. She never looked back.

All of the ill – gotten gain Frank had accumulated was in that checkbook and wallet. If Granny had known where it came from she would have tossed it out the window. All she could do was drive. When she saw the exit ramp for 'Cumberland Falls' she took it and paid for a cabin. She booked the place for one week. For six days she sat on one of the many wooden benches behind the iron railings overlooking the falls the town was named for. The place had a variety of places to eat so there wasn't any need to leave. She looked for answers in the waterfalls and the powerful wet currents and mists that went up to heaven. On night six she prayed – "Oh God, my powerful deliverer and redeemer. You have made me a new Earth in just six days. Where, Father of time and creation, do I go from here? What do I do?"

The sun had set while Granny was praying, and there in the presence of God and the rushing waters of the falls, she witnessed a 'moonbow' created from the full moon and the mist. She knew what to do. She had heard Frank talk of Indiana, so she would seek her comfort there, north of Indianapolis in the cornfields of the Hoosier state. And on day seven, she left the state of Kentucky and never returned. The Sheriff had ruled Frank's death an accidental shooting while cleaning his gun, so no one sought Granny. It was easy, then to just let the earth claim the trailer. She didn't need it, the money from selling it, or the memories it held.

That's how Granny found herself in the corner of the balcony of the church where the Pastor of Howard County was preaching that day. She always felt it was the whispering of the Holy Spirit of God that told her to turn west as she passed through the little town, so she turned off the paved county road. Frank could not reach her there, or anywhere else.

The Pastor would never be able to recall just what song Jane had chosen to play for their benediction that day, but he would always remember the sight of the lone woman on the back row of the balcony when she stepped out and slowly made her way to the front of the church. Her walk down the aisle reminded him of a wedding day when the bride walked toward her future. No one was there to walk her down the aisle, but she came anyway. All the while that the visitor made her way to the front, the church pastor thought of Granny from the 'Beverly Hillbillies'. If ever there was an exact twin to the character in the black and white television series it was the person making her way toward her own destiny.

There was no baptism that day but after a solid week of counseling between Granny and the preacher there was one the following Sunday. As Granny came up out of the rivers of life and washed away the guilt of Frank the congregation sang **"Now I belong to Jesus"**, *Jesus belongs to me. Not for the years of time alone, but for eternity"*, (Norman J. Clayton b. 1903). The people witnessing the scene clapped and shouted. The sign out front of the old church said nothing about this being a charismatic congregation, but strangely, that day it was. And the people knew just what else they were going to do. They would purchase the house at 301 Wickersham and begin to beat back the darkness of homelessness – one family at a time. And that's exactly what they did.

Everyone in the congregation contributed something once the transactions had been completed between buyer and seller, realtor and banker, title company and Howard County courthouse. The ladies hung new valances and curtains and lined the kitchen cabinets and drawers. Tim brought his bobcat loader and graded the gravel driveway. Sue decorated each room with fresh cut flowers from her garden and Alice, the little girl who daydreamed of decorating one of the bedrooms with her dolls, did indeed do so. Her own quilt, depicting an embroidered watering can that poured flowers, was embroidered into it and Alice prayed that the room would be watered with love for whoever resided there.

The lights were always on at 301Wickersham. It seemed that Granny never slept. She did what she did best, accepting and serving the children of the little town. She baked, she gardened, she made quilts for the poor. Most people thought she was just devoid of any need for sleep. The truth – she avoided it – she always dreamed of the last night she saw Frank, so she prayed. "Dear Father in heaven, my faithful Jesus, please take away my memories, I simply cannot Bear them."

"Be careful what you ask for child." Granny heard the voice of her mother speak to her from her childhood once again. "God can always help His children, but the passage may not be as easy as you think."

"I can't help it mom, I just cannot bear the memories."

Granny wasn't at the 'parsonage' long as fate would have it. After all the beatings at the hands of Frank, she started forgetting. One piece of memory after another fell like golden leaves in Autumn. The Pastor arranged to have someone live there with Granny during the last days she spent on earth. The doctors had confirmed it – Alzheimer's. It has been said that the disease was a thief because it took away ones memories. In Granny's case – it was a *'Generous Thief'*.

God did answer Granny's prayer. She forgot Frank and the awful passage that brought her to her peaceful end, but she never did forget 'The Pastor of Howard County'. He was the only leaf remaining on the tree of her memories. He would regularly stop to visit with Granny before going to his own home. Only the pastor knew the whole story about Granny's past. After his final visit to say good-bye to Granny he closed the Hobbit door behind him and noticed his own reflection in the storm door glass. He turned and walked down the few steps and short sidewalk that led away from 'the parsonage'. He faced the sun and felt a faint warmth on an otherwise cool fall day. The glass door's reflection of the retreating pastor continued to study the back of the middle aged man. Shocks of gray were playing at the man's temples. Time and burden had begun to chisel at the stolid shoulders of a man that had already born great weight. More would be exacted from the pastor. More would be required. But for the moment, The Pastor of Howard County looked at one of the most dazzling Hoosier sunsets, breathed in the clean cool of the evening and walked away.

The pastor's reflection however, remained, and watched the pastor go, then ever so slowly it slipped back into *'The House of Spirits'*.

Chapter Two

TO HELL AND BACK –
A TALE OF TWO GRAVES

*D*arkness – pitch black as vile ink and endless; yet he could see with only his senses beyond his sarcophagus – but how? He was entombed in a space so small he could not move. The cramped tomb sat on an ancient dais surrounded by ancient stone columns. His legs were gone so he could not kick at his confines. He possessed no tongue or lungs so screaming was impossible – no arms to lift up against the lid and no eyes to see with – he had only his senses. He was a victim of his circumstances; circumstances that could not be changed. Noises scratched and clawed at the small box – noises belonging to something inhuman that wanted so desperately to have him but what terrified him most was the presence at the back of the platform – waiting. It was something that was content to wait – it *patiently waited...*

Two men living at opposite corners of Howard County with seemingly nothing in common suddenly had more in common than either man would have wished. Their reaction to the night terror was the same – abject horror. Each sat on the edge of his bed, head in hand, while the body of each man shook as if caught outside in a winter storm with nothing to protect him from the biting cold. Neither man knew what to call the experience, but it was for both a confrontation with truth. It was far too vivid and real to be just a dream. In the corners of their mind the truth screamed at them like the harsh north wind - they had been **'To Hell and Back'**.

The' *Pastor of Howard County'* once said in a Sunday sermon that "if mankind could spend just three minutes in Heaven there would be no more sin. If mankind could spend just three minutes in hell, there would be no more apathy." Neither man had been present to hear the pastor's sermon, but their wives were.

Theodosius Aloysius Baxter the third – Theo, was the son of two eccentric hippies. The naming of their one and only son was only one of many eccentric things they had done in life. Theo, like his parents, belonged to the 'arts crowd'. Theo's specialty was metals. If it involved the forming, molding, hammering, or creating anything out of common or rare metals Theo was the man. His work was admired throughout the central United States and his shop in rural Howard County was well known among and frequented by any who appreciated fine craftsmanship. Unique lamps were what he liked to make the most.

'Diver Dan' wasn't for sale, however. This lamp sat behind the front desk of Theo's shop on a hand – carved mantel. Waves of the sea and froth and exotic mermaids that surfaced and dived were carved all over the oak mantle. Huge amounts of money were offered for 'Diver Dan' to no avail. Instead of a lamp shade, Theo had hammered a diver's helmet out of polished brass, with fine beads of lead to frame the face shield. Deep within the helmet were two small red lamps that gave the impression of a sinister presence – a premonition as it would turn out.

Katrina Koran Conrad – Karen, like Theo, felt her parents had gone 'off the rails' in her naming. She was content to simply be 'Karen'. She met Theo at an Ivy League school out east and was attracted by the brooding, introspective, artist and thinker. Karen sought answers to life's questions in literature. While in college she read anything that purported to give answers to the quandaries of life. It was a puzzle to Theo as to why Karen had settled on such a simple solution to so many complex and troublesome questions about humankind's existence – *"In the beginning was the Word, and the Word was with God. He was with God in the beginning. Through him all things were made; without him nothing was made that has been made. In him was life, and that life was the light of men. The light shines in the darkness, but the darkness has not understood it."* (John 1:1-5 NIV)

To Karen, the Apostle John was a poet, and these lines of thought were clean and simple. God had made everything and used His own son to reach out to humankind. It was simply up to humankind to render a response. But Theo would rather 'contemplate' and discuss the deep meanings of life during their many 'fireside chats'. Karen would pour herself a glass of sweet tea while Theo opted for a serving of Kentucky made bourbon that he procured from a quaint little restaurant in Little Nashville, Indiana just outside of Bloomington. He ran into the delivery man once who boasted of the deep flavor. The driver in bib overalls had made a lifelong customer and a slave to its effects.

"The effect of sin is like ripples in a still pond. Toss a rock and the ripples of water go on and on. Our actions in life affect so man." The Pastor of Howard County had once said these words in a sermon that most had forgotten – but not Karen. She did not pass judgement on her flawed artist companion though. She simply passed on to him the words of life and painted on the canvas of Theo's thoughts – when he would listen.

Theo needed Karen as much as he needed air to breathe. She was lithe and veritably danced on air when she walked. If ever the elves walked on earth she was a descendant. He remembered seeing her for the first time – it was love at first sight. Theo had asked a friend if there were any interesting freshmen on campus and Karen's name was dropped. Theo was on his way out the doors of the Social Science building when Cindy came around the corner with Karen. "Hey Theo! This is Karen!" She was embarrassed to death but both Theo and Karen knew – they had just met their future.

When they graduated, they married and decided to start life in the corn fields of central Indiana. The thought of it reminded Karen of living in the Shire where the madness of the coasts only flew overhead on their way to other madness. Karen was a writer. It didn't matter much where she chose to live and an artist like Theo had people come to him. They had intended to have children but never got around to it. They loved life and each other and that had always seemed enough and would probably have proved to be so had fate not stepped in.

Katrina Koran Conrad passed away at the Saint Joseph Hospital in Kokomo, Indiana on a peaceful and sunny Sunday afternoon in the presence of a broken and brooding artist and The Pastor of Howard County. She didn't see the semi that ran the red light on Highway 31 on her way home from the Church of Christ at the far end of North Main Street. "Nothing for a Christian is an accident", she whispered to her husband through the fog of the morphine iv drip. Karen was the one doing the comforting. "I'm still on my way home."

Her parting request to her pastor was for him to look in on her husband every Sunday afternoon because Theo needed to find *his* way home, too - to *her* and to her dear friend and Savior. She was buried in the same sun dress with flowers that reminded Theo of summer and sandals that she so often wore to Church. Then the weekly visitations by the pastor began. Every Sunday afternoon at about the same time of day that his dear Karen had died, the pastor asked if Theo was ready to accept The Lord. Theo's response was always the same. He politely declined the invitation, withdrawing farther and farther into the golden bottles of Kentucky bourbon.

Disappointed people traveled from the far reaches of Michigan, Ohio, and Minnesota to visit the famous artist's shop amid the cornfields of rural Howard County, only to find a 'CLOSED' sign posted on the door. The artist in Theo, and Theo himself, were slipping away – so in an act of painful compassion the dreams began.

At the age of two, the boy's parents purchased him a green and yellow John Deere pedal tractor to ride up and down their long paved driveway. He would travel back and forth between the front door and the mail box on the hot asphalt until he was exhausted and dripping with sweat from the bill of his John Deere cap to the soles of his tiny little feet. For his fourth birthday he was given a set of red cast aluminum Allis Chalmers farm implements. He would played with them on the floor of his living room as he watched 'Bonanza'. He loved Hoss with his big ten gallon hat, Adam in all black, and Little Joe too, but he wanted most to be Ben – the man in charge. When he was twelve he helped his father bail hay until his skin became so tanned and dark that he looked like a Native American Indian fresh off the reservation. On his eighteenth birthday he purchased his own tractor which his father co – signed for without hesitation. Ben Cartwright wasn't his real name but everyone who knew the kid called him 'Ben' because of his fascination with farming and ranching and 'The Ponderosa'. "Someday I will own my own Ponderosa", Ben promised himself - and he did.

It wasn't as if Ben had no other interests in life nor that he couldn't have been a good athlete in high school had he chosen to be one – he just didn't want to. He loved base-ball though. The radio in his navy blue and silver Dodge Ram 3500 Cummins diesel was always tuned to the only team in central Indiana that was forbidden – the Saint Louis Cardinals. "Who doesn't like Bob Gibson, Curt Flood and Lou Brock", Ben would argue. In high school Ben would don his blue corduroy FFA jacket over a flam-boyant red shirt in honor of his Cardinals. The only thing that changed over the years was the FFA jacket with the big gold emblem emblazoned on the back – the flaming red polo remained.

Another of Ben's lifelong interests was Martha McCutchen. They met in FFA and if one of them was seen anywhere at school or in town the other could be found somewhere nearby as well. They were inseparable. Ben and Martha were destined to walk hand in hand throughout their long life together and everyone knew it. Nothing about Martha was small. She was a beautiful red haired raw boned farm girl. "Go big or go home", was her motto throughout life and it did not change from the time she first took two steps instead of just one until the time she turned old and gray and could no longer walk at all.

Ben and Martha were a pair of mismatched socks, but for all their differences they were still paired together. Where Ben loved the Cardinals, Martha loved the Cubbies so each summer they would visit Wrigley Field in Chicago, where Martha would sport her white shirt with the blue pin stripes and in the Fall they would travel to Saint Louis to see the arch and take in a game at Busch Stadium, which was just as well since the Cardinals were always in contention by fall. The Cubbies were not. No matter which stadium they attended, the leather lungs of Martha could be heard from one end of the baseball field to the other. *"Go big or go home!"*

The other place where Martha made her vocal presence known was in church. She sang in the choir and belted out her deep vibrato to the absolute joy of the congregation. Each Christmas season people from across the county would attend the Festival of Jesus' Birth conducted at the Church of Christ at the far end of north Main Street. One of the big attractions was the acapella solo by Martha McCutchen singing "Sweet Little Jesus Boy" (Robert MacGimsey 1934). A dry eye could not be found in the house by the time she finished, and on the back row one could always find Ben – a stranger to the confines of church attendance normally, but his wife's song always touched his heart – the part where Martha lived. There just wasn't any 'room in the Inn' left for "The Sweet Little Jesus Boy" in the other chambers of Ben's heart. Ben only had room for two things in his life – Martha and 'The Ponderosa'.

"...TOMORROW YOU DIE" ((Luke 12:16-21) (Matthew 16:26b) (2 Peter 2:7)

The Pastor of Howard County delivered a three point sermon, and once it was delivered no one clapped: no one said amen: no one so much as breathed. Martha McCutchen listened, squirmed, wrung her sweating hands, and prayed for her beloved Ben. The Pastor was talking to a man who was not there to hear the message and it frightened her soul.

I. The Gain(Luke 12: 16-21)***"What would you give for the world?"***
"...I have never met a contented rich man. Like Alexander the Great he cries for more..."

II. The Exchange(Matthew 16: 26b)***"What would you give for your soul?"***
"...you are penniless: powerless to make this transaction – you have no credit here..."

III. The Loss(2 Peter 2:7)***"What would you give to take it all back?"***
"...all of your worldly gain was merely a mirage: a distraction. Behold – it is gone!..."

The musicians were supposed to play the benediction that day – it said so in the bulletin; but they couldn't. No one moved. The sermon hung in the air and the Holy Spirit

of God hovered there, and the people were greatly con-
victed. So, in the silence, the lone man on the stage sang
the benediction. The pastor sang in a cracking voice that
betrayed the depths of his emotions. And the people cried.

Ben thought he had used his time wisely while Martha
was attending Sunday morning church service. Since it
was a day of worship, the hired hands were gone, and it
was just the owner of the 'Ponderosa' who worked. The
demands of a mega farm were seven days a week for
Ben – the boss – just like he had planned ever since he
straddled himself over the seat of that little John Deere
pedal tractor so many years prior. Combines number four
and five needed an oil change and number one required a
GPS update on its software. He had intended to move the
water rigs over to field number eight, but an early morning
thunder storm had checked that task off his to – do list for
him. He sat on a stone bench at the top of 'The Mount of
Olives' looking out upon hundreds of acres of corn, soy
beans and milo. Martha was the one who named the spot.
She said it reminded her of the place where Jesus would
take refuge and think. Every morning, she could be found
there with her Bible and devotional before the morning
chores began.

Martha McCutchen drove her fully restored Ford
Bronco up the long lane that led to their massive farm
house in the trees. The Bronco was brought back to life
by her husband as a Christmas present. She could have
driven a more modern mode of transportation, but it had
belonged to her dad. He was gone, but his presence could

always be found in that old Bronco. She knew where her Ben would be – 'The Mount of Olives' - because he said it reminded him of her. So, she changed into her riding clothes and went to the horse barn and saddled up 'Rusty' - her palomino, to go and find her Ben. Martha was still distressed over the morning service, and she was searching for a way to reach her husband's heart for the eternal – again. So she prayed, not thoughtlessly but earnestly.

"Oh, my precious brother, when the world's on fire, you'll need my Jesus to be your Savior. He'll hide you ever, in the rock of ages. In the rock of ages – just cleft for you." The Pastor had sung with emotion these words for the benediction that morning when no one came to his rescue, and the song had remained in Martha's mind. She was afraid for her Ben and the premonitions would not go away. She was afraid of fire, and the thought of her precious Ben getting caught up in the final conflagration terrified her beyond what mere words could express.

Martha McCutchen found her Ben right where she knew he would be – on the 'Mount of Olives' thinking about her. She tied the reins of her horse to the iron hitching post Ben had cemented into the ground just for her, and they sat, hand in calloused hand. They silently watched the darkened northern sky and heard distant rumblings of thunder with traces of lightning as the storm worked its way to a far - off place.

Martha broached the topic of God, salvation, and the need for every human soul to come to the point of repentance, but it did no good. Ben stood up and patted his back pocket where his thick wallet was. "This is my god. Every time I need something I just ask king George, Benjamin and Thomas Jefferson and they deliver. Don't worry about me Martha, I'll be fine." Ben didn't intend to be offensive; he was trying to be humorous, and light hearted but he had inadvertently taken off the gloves and challenged the Spirit of the one Holy God – not the one made of green paper that could be found in Ben's wallet and Martha knew the moment for what it was. Her stomach tightened into a knot and felt the ire of the Holy Spirit inside her react to what was just spoken. It was a Nebuchadnezzar moment, and the moment could not be taken back.

That night, as the mismatched but loving couple lay in bed Martha could hear her husband moan and toss in his sleep. She leaned over and gently wiped the beads of sweat from the brow of Ben and pondered – "what could my dear Ben be dreaming about?"

Once the shaking stopped the heaving started. Theo sat on the edge of the bed with his head in his hands and dabbed at his mouth with a cool wash cloth that came back soaked in blood. He used a three legged cane and got back to his aching swollen feet, went into the bathroom, and the man who looked back from the mirror was unrecognizable. His once youthful face was jaundiced and yellow as well as the whites of his puffy eyes. Red veins shot across them like red lightning across a sky of yellow. His liver was failing just as the doctors had told him. Theo always drank too much, but with the loss of Karen he all but lived in the bottle of his favorite alcohol. The loss of her was something Theo just could not overcome.

The house was empty and devoid of any noise. That is how it always was since Karen's accident. "Accident – what a strange word for something that destroys lives", mused the once artist. Theo poured himself a hot cup of coffee from a kitchen that resembled a recycle land-fill of cardboard boxes and empty plastic water bottles from takeout drive through, and microwave meals. There wasn't a woman in his life to guide him. He walked the house in silence. He probably wasn't supposed to have the coffee either but at such a point in his life "what dif-ference does it make anyway", Theo reasoned. He used a cane and walked slowly from room to room, seeing only remnants of Katrina Koran Conrad. Her art room had a potter's wheel on which sat a slab of unfinished clay. In the garage was her work station where Karen had been building kites for the kids she taught in Sunday School. String and colored markers lay unattended. Boxes of her clothes still sat in the hall waiting to go to Good Will, but Theo just didn't *have the will* to take them. So they sat in the hall collecting undisturbed dust waiting for an appro-priate time that was never to be.

The little room at the back of the old rambling farm house was where she had spent most of her free time, where she wrote articles and novels. "It's *my* 'War Room'

", she had told him. Loose pages from a partially - completed manuscript covered her writing desk while crumpled and discarded pages filled an unemptied trash can nearby. It had been her own sanctuary, where she prepared her lessons for the kids at Church and where she read her Bible. It was an unusual and somewhat wicked thing to Theo that he could still catch a faint hint of Karen's favorite perfume – the same fragrance she had used since their days in college together. It teased at his senses that she was still there, and he reflected on when they had first met. Theo replayed the scene in his mind. He reverently stepped over her afghan that lay on the floor in front of the kneeling bench that he had built for her. That is where she prayed – it's where she prayed for Theo, and Theo broke down. "Dear God, I cannot do this anymore, I simply cannot bear the silence and pain just to end up in a concrete box the size of a suitcase – show me the way out, show me how to get home – to my Karen and to you." It was then that the doorbell rang. It wasn't the usual Sunday afternoon meeting time, but it was the Pastor of Howard County just the same, coming to check on Theo.

Like Theo, Ben sat on the edge of his four posted bed with his head in his hands trying to forget. He had procured a bath towel and was wiping the sweat from his wracking body. "It was just a dream – right?" He made a poor attempt at consoling himself. It was still dark outside, but Martha wasn't in bed. It was okay though; Ben knew where she would be.

An early morning dose of double espresso, some toaster waffles, and microwave bacon might possibly chase away the night's horror, so Ben moved into their open kitchen and attempted to concoct a malady to end his troubles. He took his breakfast tray and moved outside onto the massive balcony deck that overlooked 'The Ponderosa'. The view was breathtaking. The still full moon shone heavy on the rolling acres of manicured crops that glistened in the morning dew. Off to the south of their estate up on the hill, covered in trees, the shape of Martha's palomino could be seen against the retreating clouds of the early morning, tied to the iron hitching post on 'The Mount of Olives'. Martha McCutchen wasn't sitting on the bench reading her devotional like normal. She was kneeling at the concrete bench, her alter, with her back to her home; praying. "Praying for me undoubtedly", Ben knew in his heart.

Ben sat at the black wrought iron table and chairs in the soft but diminishing ambience of the solar lights mounted on the tops of the railing posts of the deck and he waited for the morning sun to rise. Early autumn had arrived in central Indiana, and harvest had already begun. He would have a full day of work ahead of him and would have to face it with less energy than the day would require of him. The hired hands would already be in the tractor barn preparing for the day's labor. So, he made himself another cup of double espresso – "enough to keep an old elephant like me on my feet for the day", he told himself. Ben made it as far as the living room which looked out on the spacious deck. Through the wall of glass that rose to a vaulted peak of posts and polished roughhewn beams in the center of the room, Ben waited for the morning sun to rise - and rise it did. "Just like always". Ben comforted himself on the consistency of life and the never ending revolving of the seasons. No matter what his fears, life would go on like always – just as the little boy on the pedal tractor knew it would.

As Ben sat there in the comfort of his overstuffed soft brown leather chair, the sun crept over the eastern ridge of the rolling fields just as it had always done before, touching the tips of the changing leaves illuminating traces of gold, red, orange, and brown. In the comfort of that moment his eyelids began to gain weight, and so did the half consumed cup of brown energy in his right hand which slowly rolled through his fingers and fell to the floor. Ben drifted back to sleep. Like a vacuum that pulls smoke to a place it did not want to be, he was being pulled back to his night's vision of what was to become of him if the events in his life remained unaltered. Ben was back in the box.

Everything in the dream seemed just as it was a short time before, but Ben noticed something he had missed before. In the hopelessness of the situation he still had control of his mind and what was in his heart. He took consolation there and focused. "I can beat this" he told himself. "I can think myself out of this!" Then something new occurred. The floor of the small concrete box opened up and Ben could see the 'Ponderosa' in its full grand glory and Ben knew he had beaten the dream. But the acres of crops, the barns of machinery, the silos of grain, and the magnificent home caught fire and flames rose to the concrete box on the dais where his body was and began to consume him. In the mind that he was using to escape the control of his situation there was only screaming. The pain was excruciating. Then the lid of his prison came off and the monsters were there – not to take him away as he had thought. They were pushing him down – ever downward into the fires of his prosperity. Ben was being burned alive by the very thing he valued most in life – *'The Ponderosa'!*

"…all of your worldly gain was merely a mirage: a distraction. Behold – it is gone!…"

Martha had told him about the sermon which the 'Pastor of Howard County' had delivered, and the words echoed there amidst the screaming of his mind and the madness of his pain.

Ben screamed the words in his mind over and over and over – "Call the Pastor, call the Pastor, call the Pastor!!!!!!!!!!!!!!!!!!" until he could hear the voice of Martha calling *through* the pain *and* the flames and his eyes opened to see her there hovering over her Ben with a wet washcloth calling him back from hell, but Ben never stopped screaming – ***"Call the Pastor, call the pastor, call the Pastor…!"*** – so she did.

It was a mutual decision made between Theo and The Pastor that he should move into 'the parsonage' located behind the Church at the far north end of Main Street. There they would employ the hospice services for the artist during his transition between his earthly home and an eternal one. The ladies of the Church would bring casseroles and help in the care of their new house guest. And in the final days of Theo's transition between homes, an unlikely friendship was forged between two men who had lived at the opposite ends of Howard County and once had nothing in common – an artist and a rough old farmer. As fate would have it, they had an unusual connection that created a special bond of spiritual significance.

Ben visited Theo every day remaining for the artist, and the rough old farmer did something completely out of character to him – he would sing to his new friend, bringing them both peace and drawing them closer to their Heavenly Father – their forgiver and healer. 'The Ponderosa' had always been filled with the singing of Martha and Ben grew to love one of the old hymns that she would sing – "When I Survey the Wonderous Cross" (Isaac Watts 1674-1748).

One thing remained that Theo the artist needed to resolve, so after the pastor had delivered one of his more powerful Sunday messages, the elders of the Church retrieved Theo from the parsonage. Stan, Mark, Jay, Justin,

Chris, Tim, Billy, and Jared carried Theo on a hospital gurney to the sanctuary of the church, where the watery grave of baptism awaited him. The pastor, Theo, Martha, and her beloved Ben all went down into the baptistry together. They all helped lower the failing body of Theo into the water, then Ben took his own turn being buried in the waters of life. As he arose, Martha bellowed out in the most powerful performance of her life – "Now I belong to Jesus" (Norman J. Clayton, b.1903).

It was a ' *tale of two graves*' that the congregation never forgot.

Later that night Theo and Ben dreamed again. Ben stood on the white sands of a gulf that looked out onto crystal blue waters washing calmly to the shore. The coastline of the gulf he faced was ringed with palm trees that swayed gently in the breeze. He stood there taking in the peace of the place and knew that the golden streets of The Emerald City of God were somewhere behind him- forbidden to look upon until it was his time to enter its gates. Then he noticed two figures off in the distance, side by side and deep in conversation. The smaller and more lean figure was easily recognizable. The long sandy hair tied back with a leather band belonged to his newly acquired friend – Theo. He was healed and healthy. The figure beside him was a muscular Hebrew in fine white linen and dark wavy hair that fell to his shoulders. The Hebrew turned and looked at Ben with brilliant blue eyes that made contact with his own and with an imperceptible nod, the figure conveyed to Ben that it was time for him to go home – but Theo would remain.

Theo died at peace in 'the parsonage' under the comfort of a homemade quilt showing the picture of a little girl and a watering can, watering the earth with wildflowers. The same eight elders that had carried Theo to his first grave took him to his second, and after the graveside ceremony had concluded, one man with the bearing of a Ben Cartwright, stayed behind and sang to him. "…*were the whole realm of nature mine, that were a present far too small; love so amazing so divine, demands my soul, my life, my all.*" (Isaac Watts, 1674 – 1748). At his feet was a child's watering can that was filled with tenderly fresh cut wildflowers, placed there by a child from the church.

Theo had only brought a few personal possessions with him when he had moved into 'the parsonage'. An oak mantle carved with waves of the sea and froth and exotic mermaids that surfaced and dived all along the face of the wood had been mounted to the living room wall. Nestled safely on the mantle was 'Diver Dan'. The sinister red lamps had been replaced with two dazzling blue lights inside the diving helmet. Theo had said that the color blue reminded him of Heaven – and it was Karen's favorite color. Mounted on the base of the artists creativity was a new brass plate with the phrase – ***"Diver Dan, swim home to me'"*– Karen**. Which he did.

The Pastor of Howard County walked from room to room in 'the parsonage', recounting the many fond memories that were already piling up. It seemed only appropriate to him to leave the lights on inside the helmet of' Diver Dan'. The Pastor reverently pulled the door closed and he noticed how the powerful blue lights lit up the living room as the diver looked ever for his owner. And as 'The Pastor of Howard County' made his way back to his church office, he thought he could hear the faint but unmistakable sound of singing coming from *'The House of Spirits'*.

Chapter Three

A Blind Eye & Seeds of Truth

I sabell's Ford Country Squire LTD with wood grain side panels reminded one of an ancient yacht in dry dock as it sat outside the simple world war two vintage bungalow on a gravel driveway. Isabell, the seasoned saint, had something in common with her old station wagon – age. Just as an old ship with barnacles from too many days at sea there was rust from the chrome luggage racks mounted on the roof of the station wagon down to the fenders and wheel wells. Isabell and the car had both seen more than their fair share of winters over the years. The car's tan and brown vinyl interior seats had been designed to look like a cowboy belt that had been branded and tooled with bar 'S' and western motif. On cold winter months those worn and weathered seats were so stiff she gained another three inches of height before the heater softened the vinyl enough for her to sit comfortably. The radio looked new because she never touched it. Volume and station controls always remained the same.

Whomever was preaching or singing on the local Christian AM station was good enough for her. It may have been an old ride, but to this owner, it was like the cross of Jesus mounted on four weather beaten tires – a means of salvation offered to the children she would take to church each Sunday morning. Children like Charlette Ann. That was her ministry.

Like Isabell, the circuit preacher of Brown County was old but not as old as the hilly country he traveled, planting churches in towns like Story and Nashville.. The land had been purchased from the Miami Nation in the Treaty of Fort Wayne and became home to rugged Scotts – Irish living in rough cabins throughout the forested Hoosier hills. The dirt lanes and winding back roads were the ragged canvas of his life's work – planting *'seeds of truth'*. He had planted seeds from the word of God and watered the soil of his parishioners hearts with love and constant prayer.

A young apprentice traveled with him – his Timothy – who watched and learned, forming his own Christian character. The young pastor assisted the aged circuit rider by ministering to young people not much younger than himself. The younger man would eventually move north to tend his own flock and become The Pastor of Howard County, but not before one last harvest with the old preacher.

One last planting - the little white church with the red metal roof would be their last ministry together as mentor and journeyman. Their time together was short once the Church of Louisburg was established but Sir Isaac Newton was correct – for every action there is an equal and opposite reaction. The ripples of what happened there In Louisburg would go on for decades and that harvest would never stop coming in.

In times of reflection when their world would slow down and allow for such, the old circuit preacher and his apprentice would look back on the forming of that little Church in Louisburg. They would think about that middle aged Scottish woman, Isabell, with flaming red hair who owned an extremely old station wagon and a twelve year old girl – Charlotte Ann. Isabelle and the self – appointed youth minister had a heart for the people that their society had turned a blind eye to – the impoverished children of Brown County. The first child that assumed their dream was Charlotte Anne. If the word poverty could be used in conjunction with a person's name it was Charlotte Anne. She lived with her parents in a mobile home that was nestled in a thick grove of scrub oak and apple trees at the end of a rutted dirt road. Scrap sheets of plywood and parts of wooden crates made up a side walk to their front door. Seats from salvaged cars provided seating for the family. A car seat from an old Buick, a back seat from a Dodge truck, and a high - backed arm chair from an Oldsmobile minivan occupied the trailer's otherwise bare living room floor.

"I remember the first time I was in that trailer," The Pastor of Howard County later told a reporter from The Kokomo "Tribune" during an interview. "I sank down so far to the floor in one of those battered car seats that I could barely see Charlotte Anne over my knees which were completely obscuring my vision. I actually remember more of the blue corn rows of my corduroy trousers than I do about Charlotte and her family," The Pastor laughed. His stories of the founding of the Louisburg Church, Isabelle and Charlotte Anne and the incredible journey that took place there had become folklore to his congregation and the press wanted to share these stories with its Howard County readers.

Charlotte Anne was like a spark to dry tinder and she ignited a giant flame at Louisburg. She knew every child on her school bus by name and she took full advantage of it. She sat at her humble kitchen table after school and used her school supplies to create special and sincere invitations to youth group and then she handed them out the next day. She went from seat to seat on that bus handing out her hand crafted invitations with sincerity and warmth. Not a single child who boarded for school stepped off the bus without one of those invitations. And Charlotte Ann, the beautiful blond haired and blue eyed girl with a personality to warm the heart, convinced the entire school to come to her youth group meetings on Sunday night, led by the young youth minister. Her new youth leader had said that every one of God's children is born with a special gift – "you just have to find it." She had found hers – evangelism.

Charlotte Anne was the spark and Isabelle was the delivery agent. The station wagon was always full of kids going to church in the old Ford singing church songs that they had learned from the young minister. The station wagon bounced up and down and the kids hung on for dear life while singing at the top of their lungs. Isabell didn't need her radio on during those trips. Music coming from the children warmed her heart far more than anything she had ever encountered on the radio; besides, no one could have heard the radio anyway above clamor of the children. In short order her yacht on wheels could not contain the interest of so many children wanting to spend time at the Louisburg Church. On Sunday night, old cars and beat - up work trucks would show up and drop off their children. Many of those same parents decided to stay for the sermons from the old circuit preacher while waiting for their kids, who were in the capable hands of the young Timothy. It wasn't unusual to see a muddy field tractor chugging up to the church pulling a hay wagon full of kids from nearby farms. Attendance which started out as nonexistent soon became uncontainable as the flame of faith caught fire.

The young apprentice taught the kids and Isabelle played the piano – and that was enough. Toddlers sat on the laps of teen age girls and boys. Kids of all ages sat together and became one giant extended family born of a common interest and need – *koinonia* - fellowship, friendship, and family. Gathering together in the basement of that old church building provided them with a sense of community and value and purpose. Every Sunday evening was the same; a pot luck meal, games, music played from the oldest piano in Brown County and lessons from The Word of God. The young minister made it come to life and the end result looked like an episode from "The Walton's" on Walton Mountain. None who attended there, young or old, would later recount a time in their lives when they felt more at home – or at peace.

On special occasions the old circuit preacher, Isabelle and The Youth Pastor would cobble together a caravan of transport for the motley crew and travel to the big city of Cincinnati, Ohio where they would frequent the roller coasters of Kings Island. Mountain kids lived big as they screamed their lungs out on The Beast, The Banshee and The Mystic Timbers rides and eat their fill of hot dogs and cotton candy. Going home was always easy though because they had each other and that was all that mattered to them. Until...

"Grand and glorious", that's what the young pastor would say when anyone would ask him how he was doing. It wasn't grand or glorious, though, on the Sunday evening that Charlotte Anne showed up for church service with a knot on her head that was as big as a goose egg. Isabelle pulled the youth leader aside and whispered, "I've seen this before – Charlotte has a tumor."

If sidewalks and gravel for a driveway leading to a dilapidated trailer is an unaffordable luxury for a back hills family, cancer is absolutely the end of the road. The people of Louisburg were not wealthy people, but Charlotte Anne was worth saving, so the Church gathered its meager resources and sent the beautiful girl to the

K.U. Medical Center in Kansas City. The hospital specialized in cancer treatment so that is where she was sent.

The colors of fall in Brown County, Indiana were left behind in exchange for the snows and ice of Kansas City for which the place is so famous for. Charlotte Anne sat on her hospital bed, applying red nail polish when a nurse informed her that it was forbidden to have nail polish in her room, and she would need to take it off. "It's the only thing about me that's beautiful now," she sobbed. The ugly tumor had grown so large and protruded from the side of her head so that it was impossible to ignore. It was what people saw when talking to Charlotte. Her time on earth seemed short. There appeared nothing that the medical staff could do to save the girl.

Snow melts however, when the sun comes out, and the *'Son'* did come out for Charlotte Anne when the youth pastor borrowed an old Volkswagen van, loaded up the youth group and headed from the Hoosier hills to the bustling city streets of Kansas City. Little noses pressed up against the steamy windows of the van to see Christmas decorations that hung from light poles and railroad crossings. Gold bells were tucked neatly within wreaths of evergreen and multi – colored lights illuminated the ice crystals that sparkled on the sidewalks. Car horns and shouts from frantic drivers filled the air. The children's senses were on overload. But, not as much as Charlotte Anne when she saw her people come into her hospital room. She cinched up her flimsy hospital gown by the thin cotton ties and hugged each person as if it were her last time to see them – and it should have been – but it wasn't.

Those hillbilly kids went from room to room in that hospital singing Christmas Carols and praying for the sick as darkness claimed the streets of Kansas City. The children that Charlotte Anne called family slept on the cold tiles of her hospital room floor with their coats and jackets for blankets and pillows. They all prayed for the girl with pretty blond hair and brilliant blue eyes with the enormous tumor. On the sky bridge that overlooked the sleeping streets which connected the medical center to the parking garage, the youth pastor looked out on the nighttime traffic and the snow falling from a sky illuminated by the city's lights.

"Dear God", he prayed, "please heal Charlotte Anne." And God did.

When the nurses came in for morning rounds, and to rouse the sleeping children from Charlotte's room, the first thing they noticed was what was missing – their patient's tumor. In all the commotion that ensued the children were rustled from the floor and were all lined up in the back of the room crying, singing, and shouting – much to the annoyance of the K.U. medical staff - who were trying quite unsuccessfully to locate what was missing. The tumor was nowhere to be found and there was no logical explanation for it.

The trip home wasn't without incident. Little Randy became car sick, and the old Volkswagen had a couple of flat tires along the way. But the van did have an extra passenger on the way back that lifted the spirits of everyone aboard. The hospital dismissed Charlotte Anne; it's not possible to keep a patient who has nothing wrong with them. The beautiful blond haired, blue eyed girl sat in the back of the van painting her nails with red polish while the children sang. Charlotte Anne smiled because her red nails weren't the only thing about her life that was beautiful.

"That's quite a story," replied the young female reporter from the Kokomo "Tribune" as she attempted to conclude the interview with The Pastor of Howard County. She bore the dubious expression that can be found on the face of agnostics when confronted with something they cannot explain. She had heard such tales of miracles, but she was a product of the modern age, and things would need to be demonstrated to her before she believed. "What ever happened to Isabelle?"

"Well, that's a totally different story", he replied. "Isabelle continued to ferry the children in her barge to the Church of Louisburg, and she played the piano for Sunday night services just like she always had. But eventually she, too, became a victim of cancer. I'm afraid the story of Isabelle ended a bit different than that of Charlotte Anne. The cancer came on so quickly there wasn't anything that could be done. I remember going with the lead pastor to her room in Bloomington's nearby hospital for our last visit together. Isabelle was in so much pain. 'Just pray that I can pass away and leave this pain,' she had asked. "So, we heeded her request, and by the time we passed through the hospital's front doors to return home she was gone, quietly and peacefully."

"I can tell you believe in the power of prayer," the reporter responded – still doubtful about what she was being told. "Did you ever see Charlotte Anne again after you moved here to Howard County?"

The Pastor of Howard County leaned back in his brown leather office chair and removed his silver wire frame reading glasses, focused on a far off point in the ceiling that only he could see and became quiet. His eyes teared up ever so slightly as the play in his head moved across the theatre stage of his mind. He swiveled in his chair to hide his emotion from the girl. And even though the reporter noticed, just the same, she kept the knowledge to herself. After a few moments of reflection, he regained his composure and continued the story – once again about Charlotte Anne.

It was December in Howard County and snow was falling. The downtown Kokomo square and Highland Park were decorated, so The Pastor took the long way into town through the scenic park to see the Christmas decorations. The red and white covered bridge in the scenic park was strung with lights, and green garland was draped from one end of the old structure to the other. The glass - faced shed where Big Ben was housed was lit up so everyone who traveled through Highland Park could look at the stuffed animal. By the time Ben was put down by the vet, he weighed 5,000 pounds – the largest steer in the world. Kokomo didn't have a lot of things to boast about. Elwood Haynes of Kokomo had designed and built the first American gasoline engine car, but few people recalled that fact. The locals did know about Ben, however, so the town liked to show him off.

Each business on the downtown square displayed its own decorations. None of them matched but no one cared. The County courthouse stood sentry over the town square dressed in her Christmas best as if to bless all who came to walk the snow covered sidewalks and shop – or just look. The Pastor parked in one of the few flat parking spaces left and ambled into the Western Auto store for a quick look at the new toys brought in from the Fort Wayne buying show. His niece and nephew always received something from the Western Auto store. The proprietor and his family were regulars at the Church of Christ on the far north end of Main Street, so the pastor did his shopping there. He tried to come into the store when school was out because Betty and Billy, the owner's children, worked there. Betty usually worked the register in her white smock with the Western Auto logo on the vest pocket. Billy could be found in the basement building bicycles for Christmas. It was a warm and fun place to be, so the pastor didn't have to look hard for an excuse to visit there.

When he arrived back at the church, he sat the sacks of his purchases from town on the floor beside his desk in the office and settled in for an afternoon of inspirational writing. With his favorite Chicago Cubs coffee mug in hand full of steaming hot coffee, and a space heater under his desk to warm his cold wet shoes, he leaned back and surveyed the church's empty interior through his open study door. A well-lit Christmas tree stood tall in the foyer,hung with envelopes containing suggested gift ideas for the poor. Hopefully, by the end of service that night all the envelopes would be gone, taken by thoughtful souls who cared for the needy. Old familiar carols sung by Frank Sinatra came from an 8 – track tape player in the office and echoed through the vacant sanctuary, reminding him that he was all alone in the building. That night was the celebration of 'The Festival of Lights' and people from all over the county would be there to hear him talk about the Christmas miracle and hear Martha McCutchen sing about "The Sweet Little Jesus Boy". Thoroughly drenched in the mood of Christmas he picked up his fountain pen and was poised to touch it to paper and begin preparing his message when an apparition walked through the Church's double doors. It was Charlotte Anne.

Mailboxes that dotted the lanes and byways of Louisburg all received the Pastor of Howard County's newsletters. All of Brown County it seemed had heard about 'The Parsonage' located behind the Church on Main Street and what that little building meant to Granny and Theo as they walked from life on earth to Gods' golden shores, so it was only logical for Charlotte Anne to seek out her old youth minister when tragedy came knocking on her door once again. Charlotte had grown up and had become a striking young woman, but she was still unmistakably Charlotte Anne. Her piercing blue eyes gave her away in an instant. So too the red nail polish and the matching red head scarf. The beautiful long blond hair was gone, making it apparent that the tumor had returned.

They saw no need to state the obvious, the condition of Charlotte Anne was apparent. Both parties had been in that situation together before, so Charlotte sat in one of the high backed chairs in front of the pastor's desk and caught up on old times. They spoke about the youth trips to Kings Island in Cincinnati, and Charlotte told the pastor about each of the children of the old youth group and what they were doing with their lives. They spoke fondly of Isabelle and her old station wagon that had hauled so many kids to their Sunday evening services and how the poor people of Louisburg would load the back of the Circuit Preacher's Volkswagen bus with dead chickens and garden produce – mostly zucchini. The youth leader had always hated zucchini and continued to do so. The Circuit Preacher's wife had done as much with the hated vegetable as she could - zucchini bread, zucchini pudding. She cut zucchini up and placed it in vegetable soup which they always managed to push aside with their spoon as they ate their soup. Faces were carved in zucchini in October instead of pumpkins. It had been rumored among the parishioners of Louisburg that the Preacher and his wife had taken some of the smaller and more colorful gourds and sprayed them with lacquer, using them for a center piece on their kitchen table. It apparently worked out quite nicely until the gourds rotted and infested the kitchen with gnats. Their entire house had to be fumigated. They Pastor of Howard County and Charlotte Ann laughed until they cried about all the zucchinis.

While the tears of laughter were still wet on their cheeks they turned the conversation back to the K.U. Medical Center in Kansas City and what had happened there – the long trip made by the youth group, the night of prayers, and the resulting miracle that the medical staff could not explain. The Walton's had asked God for a miracle then, but the Walton's were gone, grown, and moved on to families of their own. Times for Charlotte Anne had changed as well, and she knew it – they both knew it. She told The Pastor about her diagnosis. She was down to weeks – perhaps less.

"I know about 'The Parsonage", she confessed. "Everyone in Louisburg knows about it. Shoot, I think most of Brown County knows about it. Everyone has their back to the Red Sea at some point in their life, Pastor. I didn't cross over before, but my time has come now. It's time to cross over and I'd like to do it in your parsonage that I've read about. I'll need someone to look in on me while I take this journey. But I need one last additional favor before I'm gone…"

So, with Frank Sinatra singing "Oh Holy Night" in the background, Charlotte Anne and The Pastor agreed on her transition from this life to the next, then he laid down his pen.

There would be no need for notes that night as he inspired the masses to Christmas charity and good will to men. He would simply tell the heartwarming story of his time at Louisburg, what it meant to Charlotte Anne, and what peace on earth looks like as seen from the Father's eyes.

Charlotte walked the small hallway, kitchen and living room in a never ending circuit of fog as the cancer began to claim her thinking. Eventually she was remanded to bed. "Dear God, please find a way to save my family. I cannot bear the thought of entering your wonderful Paradise knowing they will not follow. Please find a way…"

"Whatever it takes, sweet child?" The *Word* spoke to Charlotte Anne in a soft whisper that rested on her tender heart like a gentle feather sent down from heaven.

"*Yes Father, whatever it takes…*" Charlotte Anne, who was once a twelve year old blond - haired, blue - eyed child, spoke the words, and then she was gone.

The sanctuary of the Church of Christ on the far end of Main Street was unable to contain the amount of people who had arrived for the funeral of Charlotte Anne. The people of Howard County were so moved by what they had heard on the evening of The 'Festival of Lights' they had to be there to pay their respects to their admired sister in Christ. People from Louisburg made the trip north, too, and brought gifts of dead chickens and zuc- chini for The Pastor of Howard County. They knew from his days as their youth minister how much he dearly loved their zucchini.

The elders strung long electrical cords and placed speakers outside the church building so the people who congregated on the sidewalks and in the parking lot could hear the service. He had never used a funeral service as an alter call before, but it was Charlotte Anne's final request and The Pastor had agreed to it. The title of his sermon that day was *"Whatever it Takes."*

More than thirty cars had arrived from Louisburg and Brown County on the day of the funeral: and fifteen people – all from the family of Charlotte Anne, accepted Christ as their own personal Lord and Savior. They were all baptized right there at the funeral. Charlotte Anne had received her parting wish.

The modern thinking journalist from The Kokomo "Tribune" was visibly shaken as she sat in The Pastor's office, concluding her interview, and it showed. In a voice that she barely was able to control she croaked out a simple question to the pastor – one that people with seeking hearts had been asking for two millennia. "What would God do to save someone like me?"

"Whatever it takes", was the pastor's reply.

She wrote the article about The Pastor of Howard County just like she had been sent to do but had walked away with something far more valuable than a "job well done" from her editor. She told the stories of Isabelle and the boat - like Ford station wagon and how it was used as an instrument of faith to deliver children to God. She told the story of Charlotte Anne and how sometimes we are healed to demonstrate God's power and divine ability to part The Red Sea. And she told the honest truth that eventually we are all called to cross over on dry ground and make our final journey home. The news piece was a big hit with the "Tribune's" readers. Most people in town appeared to have read it and discussed its merits for a long time to come, over biscuits and gravy or pie and coffee. The title of the article appearing in the newspaper was simply – ***"Whatever It takes."***

The Pastor of Howard County kept that article and protected it under glass in a beautiful walnut picture frame. He hung it in 'the parsonage' on a wall in the living room across from the carved mantel and' Diver Dan' where it remained until the church and the old parsonage - turned home for the homeless, were eventually abandoned.

The wood grain of the gray weathered siding of the parsonage looked like coarse channels in a parched dry riverbed, flowing toward the front doorbell, forming a knot that resembled an open mouth screaming for moisture that never came. The massive picture window took up most of the front porch. Once, people stood there and witnessed some haunting Indiana sunsets. Now the glass was cracked in a million shattered pieces, held together by some inexplicable spell. There was no one there to enjoy those Hoosier sunsets anymore but when those broken pieces of glass would catch the final rays of sunset, it was like the Fourth of July inside that old house. Rainbows of color would march across the walls and disappear in the ceiling. It was an endless loop on a reel of time but only the old, abandoned house could see the show.

A vacant wall in the empty and aged living room showed the dusty silhouette of where a picture frame had once been mounted. The final rays of sunset lit up the cracked glass of the picture window and the sun walked across the wall, throwing colors of the rainbow where the frame once hung. '*The House of Spirits*' remembered what was written in the forgotten news article, and In the softest of whispers, it spoke in The Pastor's voice – ***"Whatever it Takes…"***

Chapter Four

THE ARTIST KING

"Once upon a time in a land far, far away there was an island kingdom, fair and beautiful. Peaceful golden shores ringed in the kingdom from intruders or anyone who had not been summoned there. Palm trees, green and tall, dotted the white sands of the shore lines and swayed in the gentle breezes while quiet waves of crystal blue waters lazily washed to the shore. The foam of the caps would all but sing. The King's subjects would go there – on those peaceful shores – and gaze out upon the beautiful waters and take in the solitude that could be found there. The kingdom was filled with Castles and mansions that sat on forested hill tops and bluffs with meticulous landscapes which looked out upon the vast expanse of the lands and the ocean. There were fields of flowers of every color, size and kind. Massive oaks and redwood trees grew tall and majestic so as to reach out and touch the feathery

white clouds that passed over the kingdom. Off at a great distance stood a lighthouse that the King had placed there Himself. Its brilliant beacon rotated in a never ending circuit of invitation to the weak and weary and worn travelers whom the King had summoned to Him.

Sitting tall on top of a grassy plateau in the center of the kingdom was the palace of the King. Spires reached to the heavens and flew colorful flags. It had flying buttresses and ramparts that spanned turrets and mighty ancient stone archways: it had been there for as long as time itself. The castle of the King stood proud for the people to see and always know that their king was there watching over them and they would never be abandoned by the one they loved and admired.

In the Kings' great banquet hall there were feasts of the finest foods and all the people would attend. The King knew them all by name and walked among His people – and the people loved Him dearly – everyone except Shadowman.

Lean and strong and handsome; Shadowman stood out among the people of the island kingdom because he was so appealing to look upon but his dark curly hair and pointed beard were as dark as his sin soiled heart. He hated the king. Shadowman saw with his black eyes the fairness and beauty of the kingdom and how the King's subjects worshipped him, and he wanted to be worshipped as well. He wanted all that the King possessed for himself. Shadowman wanted the great King gone – permanently.

So, Shadowman walked the cobblestone road that led up to the King's castle. He took in the sights: gas lights that lined the road and flowers that were meticulously groomed by the gardeners of the King and instead of seeing beauty he saw only contempt. He was intent on finding the King. He was intent on doing Him harm.

Shadowman walked the halls of the castle in search of his prey but the halls were empty, and the King was nowhere to be found. His steps echoed in the cavernous palace and returned to his ears as cruel taunts that he was in someone else's home – not his. He came to a small room locked away in the farthest reaches of the Castle keep. The door was closed but that did not hinder the seeker of violence and trouble. Shadowman pushed open the door and beheld the King's creative masterpiece. It was a canvas of life; colors that the man had never seen before. The painting moved and had light of its own. Space, stars and planets; people alive and moving from edge to edge floated across the pane of vision as the scenes changed – always changing.

There was a new dimension that Shadowman had never witnessed before – time. Time gave hope that anything was possible within the painting. So Shadowman did what was forbidden to the subjects of the island kingdom – he entered the canvas of the King. "If I cannot have the island kingdom, I will have this", he reasoned.

The noises in the keep did not go unnoticed to the Prince of the kingdom who sought out the source of those sounds and saw what had happened. So, the Father's own son went into the painting to defeat Shadowman. The creator became the created in order to save creation."

"…and that is how our Michael came to know Shadowman." The Pastor of Howard County was doing what he had learned to do all the way back in Louisburg while practicing as a youth minister at the little white church with the red metal roof. It was Sunday evening and he had gathered the children together in the living room of 'The Parsonage' behind the Church of Christ at the end of Main Street. Granny, Theo, and Charlotte Anne had all passed away and no one lived there currently, so he used the building as a gathering place for the children.

He sat in a recliner with little Edith in his lap while spinning spiritual tales to explain why one of their own was there no longer.

People of the congregation had been searching for Michael for over a month. The real truth, however, was Michael had been searching for himself for a lot longer than that…

The Pastor stood at his own kitchen sink, rinsing his coffee cup from the tap, pondering Michael's tragic discovery in the woods of upstate Ohio. He was also struggling to find a way to break this news to the other children. "Life is a lot like a kitchen faucet," he thought. "The faucet has the capacity to deliver *hot* water or *cold* – it's up to the individual which comes out".

He stared at the two handled faucet that reflected his face back to himself in the polished chrome. The Pastor saw the deep lines of concern on his own face and the encroaching gray that was claiming his temples – "as bad as crabgrass," he thought sourly. He also noticed how the hot water handle on the left was clearly marked with a red dot while the cold side had a blue dot. "Every life is the same", he mused, – "choose the red dot or the blue one. Every life struggles with both until one of them is simply rusted shut from lack of use." The Pastor liked the idea of using a kitchen faucet as a sermon illustration when he addressed the entire congregation about Michael, but the whole topic of good versus evil and what happens when a person gives themselves completely over to the dark side was too deep and sinister for children. He needed to find another way to break the news to the Sunday night youth group, so he created the story of "The Artist King."

The Pastor of Howard County took his re – filled coffee cup, the cracked one bearing the logo of Kings island, and moved to his study. He seated himself in his office chair and pulled out a file from the cabinet under his desk: **SINGLE PARENT HOMES**. The statistics were staggering, and even though they tended to fluctuate the impact was consistent – devastating.

- 63% of youth suicides are from homes with no father
- 90% of all runaway youths are from homes with no father
- 71% of all high school drop outs are from homes with no father
- 70% of all youths in juvenile detention institutions are from homes with no father
- 75% of adolescent substance abuse centers are youths from homes with no father

The pastor leaned back in his chair and mentally paid his last respects to Michael. It was all he could do. "The poor boy didn't stand much of a chance," thought the preacher.

Michael had been a cute kid who grew up in the care of his single mom. She did absolutely the best she could. Working, helping Michael with homework, taking him to little league practice and youth group. The little boy was a perfect example of someone standing at the kitchen sink and taking turns as to which spigot he would turn – the hot one, or the cold one; back and forth; back and forth. He was always in trouble, usually for theft. The pastor didn't dare take a stick of gum from Michael when it was offered because there was no telling from where it came, a gift from his mother, or simply stolen from the convenient store down the street from his house. Michael didn't have any qualms about taking what was not his, but he also had no problem with giving it away.

As a young teen, Michael went to work for one of the Elders at the church and fell in love with the man's daughter. The Elder became a father figure to him, and the girl gave Michael a reason to behave. But when she broke up with Michael his world came crashing down. He wanted and needed a home and people to call a family so Michael fell in with a bunch of other troubled youths who thought it a good idea to play with tarot cards, a Ouija board, and conduct seances. They called out for attention in the clothes they wore and the tattoos that covered their arms and legs- pentagrams, daggers, and inverted crosses. Their hair was spiked and dyed neon blue or red. The boys wore black eye liner and long black leather coats, just like the girls. They all but screamed out for someone to notice them, and it did not matter if that attention was bad. In fact, they preferred negative attention as opposed to none at all because it gave credence to their preconceived assumption that no one cared for them anyway.

One night The Pastor awoke to find the Elder at the foot of his bed calling for the preacher to get up – his house was never locked. There was an emergency involving Michael. The boy had broken into an abandoned home in a bad part of town, armed with a shotgun. When the two men found Michael, he began yelling obscenities at the Elder and pastor as they approached him. A deep, sinister, disembodied voice that did not belong to the youth taunted the men. The voice from another realm cited the awful things the preacher had done in his life; things that no one could have known. Things the pastor had tried diligently to forget.

When the presence finally left Michael, he was screaming for help which was freely given. Over the following several months of counseling, the boy attained his life back – until Michael reached out once again for the proverbial kitchen faucet handle with the red dot, scalding himself permanently. Michael sought out his old friends who had helped take him down blind alleys of the mind and into behaviors that lead to destruction.

Sometimes people find themselves at exactly the wrong place at the exact wrong moment in time, where disaster strikes. That is how it was for a mother of two traveling north on U.S. 31 in the middle of the night. She had had left the I.U. Medical Center in Bloomington where her father was being treated for cancer and headed for South Bend and a warm bed for her and her two little girls. It was freezing cold outside their car so the heater fan in their sedan made a soft hum that had placed both of the children in a peaceful sleep. The mother was imagining her home, a warm meal, and an awaiting husband who had spent a long and arduous day at work. As she crossed under the overpass she did not see Michael, or his two cohorts cloaked in the darkness or the boulder they dropped over the railing of the bridge which took the lives of the three innocent travelers – the driver heading north for home and her two young passengers.

Michael stood in a crowd of people who had congregated in a nearby Waffle House parking lot which looked out upon the highway and watched as the fire department extinguished the fire and retrieved the charred bodies from the mangled mess that had blocked U.S. 31 traffic for miles in both directions. In the flashing red and blue lights that pierced the blackness, all Michael could see in his own mind was the boulder moving in slow motion as his fingers reluctantly released his tentative final grasp on the rock that had not only killed an innocent family but had sealed his own fate as well. When the Highway Patrol officer inquired of the people in the crowd just what they had seen, knowing eyes flitted toward Michael. The suspicious trooper slowly made his way through the crowd, toward Michael who panicked and bolted.

"…the Great King stood in front of His masterpiece in the castle keep and looked at the flashes of

lightning and the crashing of waves upon great rocks of the sea within the canvas walls. The din of the storms there was all but deafening. There was a mighty battle raging within the painting as The Prince of the island kingdom did battle with Shadowman. The Prince fought for the souls of men within the painting while Shadowman sought to bring them all down and spite the mighty King for hate's sake. – "My sweet boy, my sweet, sweet boy," the Artist King watched the war before Him and wept for His only Son."

Michael took the back roads of Howard County in his old Chevy truck, the one the three gang members had ridden in to get to the overpass and drove east with his lights off so the law would not follow. He drove slowly – endless mile after mile with only the light of a winter's full moon to guide him. He backtracked evasively and drove ever eastward, then eventually north once he hit the Ohio line. There in the darkness of his monotonous prison he lapsed into maniacal madness as shadows spread throughout his mind and soul like deadly cancer. When lucidity would surface, the only thing that Michael could see was the giant rock as it slid from his fingers. He saw the rock in his mind's eye as if it were only centimeters from his fingertips. He wanted to take it back – prayed to take it back – but could not. Such is the state of life when deeds are set in motion that cannot be taken back.

The oak trees that had lined the rural northern Ohio two – lane highway turned to pines as he entered the Mohican – Memorial State Forest. Hills were filled with white and red pines, aspen and hemlock trees as far as the eye could see. He found an AM Christian radio station among the static of the radio in that obscure location and attempted to find solace in it – but he could not. The voices within his mind could not be silenced. Michael parked the truck and sat on some moss covered rocks on the forested bank of the Clear Fork River that ran through the forest, seeking answers, but the only answers that came to him were the ones supplied by sources that meant Michael harm and not good. "God always provides a way out," he recalled his pastor once telling him, but Michael wasn't seeing it. The only thing Michael could see was the look of peace and satisfaction on the face of a young mother as she glanced over to admire her little girls sleeping in the passenger seat next to her before their world literally came crashing in.

Michael buried himself deeper in the folds of his black leather jacket seeking to find some comfort there, and warmth from the cold, but found little of either. He looked across the Clear Fork River and saw a doe and fawn eating what they could find. It reminded him once again of the tragic scene that never stopped playing out in his mind since he left Indiana the night before. Finally – Michael came to know a type of peace that only the troubled and tormented can know, and he knew just what to do. He reached out for the hot water spigot one last time.

The Pastor of Howard County was in his office at the Church of Christ at the end of Main Street when the call came in from the Ohio State Highway Patrol. A Park Ranger in the Mohican – Memorial State Forest had found what remained of Michael hanging from the limb of a white pine. The preacher's name and contact information were left in a parting note from Michael which was addressed to "The Pastor of Howard County". The letter expressed gratitude for all that he and his mother had done for him over his lifetime and sincere remorse for the things he had done – most of all was the loss of life at his own hands on U. S. Highway 31. The Pastor wished Michael had recognized that everyone is involved in the epic battle between good and evil. "We are all players in this play'" he mused. "There is only one way it ends well – safe in the forgiving arms of almighty Jesus."

The Ohio Patrol Officer had asked the Pastor to come and get the Chevrolet truck which had been found looking out on the bank of the Clear Fork River in the state park. He and the Elder who had become the father figure to Michael made the trip together to recover it and the other meager remnants of Michael's short life on earth. When the pastor fired up the old truck, the radio was still tuned in to a local AM Christian radio station. A song was playing through the static on Michael's radio that the preacher wished Michael had heard and taken to heart. The song spoke about the past being a closing door and that we don't live there anymore. It was a pertinent message that might possibly have saved the boy's life had he heard it in time and embraced its deep meaning.

It was a long drive back to The Pastor's home – not only in miles but in the solitude within Michael's old truck and the reality of everything that had transpired. The preacher tried to make sense of life's lessons and came away with a few rays of light – but very few. Life was simple really, and fragile. An epic battle was being played out behind the curtain of life and the stakes could not be higher. Life on earth was like living in a fish bowl to him; made of one way glass. One cannot see out but there was a very tangible reality outside that fish bowl that could see in – where the humans live. "It's hard to fight against something so real yet which cannot be seen," he thought. In the end, the Pastor concluded that life was really quite simple – just make the right choices and say you're' sorry when we mess up. "After all, isn't that why Jesus came in the first place – to forgive?" he concluded.

So, that's how little Edith came to be sitting on The Pastor's lap listening so intently to the tale of the Artist King and the island kingdom. She had listened to the story attentively and thoughtfully, with great interest in her own eyes and looked up into the eyes of The Pastor of Howard County and said: "I don't like '*Thadowman*' – heth's mean!" Edith was missing her two front teeth so pronouncing 'S' words was all but impossible for the adorable child. "Tell us about the Printh of the island kingdom!" she demanded.

"The mighty King and the Prince of the island kingdom stood in the castle keep and looked together upon the painting of creation. There were storms and sickness, disease and tears – things the Artist King had never intended to be in his painting of life – but now were there as a result of Shadowman. But there was something new in the painting that was not there in the beginning – a rope that led out of the painting and back into the island kingdom. All that was necessary for the people living in the painting was to grab the rope and they could come home – home to the King and the Prince who had saved them.

*…and as the King and Prince were standing there looking, a little white house stood out in the painting. Inside that house was a Pastor of the Word and a little girl sitting on his lap listening ever so intently to this story about the mighty King and His Son, and throughout the painting, from beginning to end, there was a quieting voice that spoke peace and promise – **"it is finished."***

Chapter Five

BABY LAND

P olished oak slats were bolted to a black wrought iron frame. A deep slash on the right arm rest went all the way down to bare metal, and a gouge in the seat made her wonder what had happened to cause it. She had the bench's features memorized and knew them like the back of her hand. This was her resting place each morning as she sat and watched over her babies. They were just ahead; each had their own white stone with their name and date written upon it. The grave markers were like tiny little teeth sticking up out of the earth. Attached to each one was a multi – colored foil whirly gig that turned lazily in the breeze and reflected the rays of the morning sun hitting the revolving blades. These were the decorations of the month. Each new month something different was featured on the headstones. When Hallie was satisfied that all her children knew they were loved she left. Driving under the massive arch that led into and out of the cemetery, she saw the scroll work and the iron letters in her rear view mirror that told where she had just been. Everything appeared to be spelled backward in her mirror, but she knew what the letters spelled just the same. This was the home of her dear ones - *' Baby Land'.*

Time. Time is like a mighty, mighty army and days are its soldiers. Those soldiers come against the fortified walls of spirit, soul and mind until resolve and stamina are depleted, leaving despair and brokenness in its wake like the ruins of a once strong castle. Such was the life of Hallie. Days, months, and years threw themselves at the walls of her dreams and hopes in a vain effort to wear her down, but she would not be dissuaded. Hallie wanted a family and would settle for nothing less, but just like Samuel's mother Hannah, God used time, disappointment, and impossibility to tell His story and His mighty power to alter the courses of time. He did so with Hallie and her child – Boston. This is their story.

Growing up, Hallie loved to climb the narrow stairs that led to her grandma's attic and rummage through an old oak chest of drawers, sitting there in the dust and dark, beside the oval window that looked out onto the back yard of her grandma's house. Hallie was certain the old chest had the answers to life. In the third drawer down was everything Hallie needed for survival: ethics, values, morals, and faith. "Just stay out of the other drawers," she could imagine her departed grandma warn her. "You won't like what you find there." It was a mental exercise she played out in her mind whenever she was looking for answers to life's dilemmas and challenges. She always found what the situation required in that dusty attic. The old piece of furniture spoke to her as if her grandmother were still alive. Society of that time went to that third drawer down and found such things as prayer, kindness, and God's Word. Hallie knew this to be true because words like 'prayer' and places such as 'church' could still be found in pop culture and in songs on the radio. A time would come however when the drawers would be taken out and all the contents dumped out on the rough, dusty floor. The drawers would be broken apart and thrown away because they were limits and people would grow to despise limits and boundaries. "Pick what you want. Pick what fits best for you and your own life, if you don't like it then don't take it. Don't judge others for what they pick up though. By all means, do not judge. " These sardonic words from her grandmother had prophesied of a world view yet to come. And now it was here.

Hallie would take from the third drawer down and apply what she found there into her own life; the lessons and life principles which molded her and formed her into the woman that could listen with a discerning heart and wait on the Lord with patience and perseverance. And perseverance was a trait that would someday mean for her the difference between despair and fortitude.

She played basketball in Junior High School. It might have seemed out of character to someone who didn't know the girl, how such a beautiful child could be so rugged and competitive. Shiny brown hair with streaks of gold, tied in a pony tail, bounced off her back as she ran down the court. If school boys followed her agile and graceful movements down the court with admiring eyes she didn't notice. She was a focused girl; someone who knew who she was and where she was going at all times.

Her own father was her coach, and The Pastor of Howard County volunteered his time as the assistant. The Pastor seemed to be everywhere at the same time – speaking from behind the pulpit, volunteering to coach athletics at the school, and counseling those who needed him – and there was always someone who needed him. With no family of his own to go home to, he filled his day with the needs and interests of others. That is what propelled him forward in life – his adopted family – the people of Howard County.

Hallie and The Pastor would reminisce together about the big game, when David was up against Goliath, her little farm community against mighty New Castle. It was an impossible task. "Untuck your shirts and go out there looking like a bunch of 'slop jars'. Take your time like you just got out of bed. Becky – go out there with your shoes untied and hold up the tip – off while you take your time tying them. I want them to think we are a bunch of hayseeds. When we get the ball, I want you to show them how wrong they are," The Pastor instructed. The arrogant kids of New Castle snickered and laughed as the motley crew of Howard County took to the court in slow motion with a seemingly defeated spirit. Goliath was completely caught off guard and didn't regain any semblance of com-posure until half – time.

With only seconds left, the game was tied. David and Goliath were at their respective benches listening intently to their coaches' instructions. The game was on the line and Howard County was only seconds away from pulling off ***"The Great Upset – David defeats Goliath"*** as the headline would appear the following day in the sports section of The Kokomo "Tribune". A play concocted by The Pastor won the game, and it was the last second shot by Hallie that drove the final nail into the coffin of mighty New Castle. The slop jars of Howard County defeated a polished machine and went on to win the State Championship that year. The team's trophy still stands in a glass case in the foyer of the main hall. Under the trophy is the photo of the girls who accomplished the impossible, and in the center of the team, kneeling with the ball, is a confident young girl with shiny brown hair – someone who knew who she was and where she was going at all times.

A thin sheet of hammered copper was affixed to a dark block of wood by four copper brads. Just why Hallie's grandmother had placed the plaque in the third drawer as a demonstration of work ethic was a puzzle to Hallie, but she studied it – and she applied the lessons that she saw there. It was an intricate rendering of a regal county courthouse with trimmed shrubs and attractive trees that sat on top of a gentle rise which looked down upon the city sidewalks full of pedestrians walking from store to store carrying shopping bags full of treasures. The house of law had large windows flanking stone arches over double doors that welcomed local citizens to its spacious corridors. Those doors stood wide open, and inside the courthouse steps was a woman of color on her hands and knees with a cleaning bucket and a scrub brush. She was hand washing the white marble steps of the building, step by step with meticulous care as men in dark suits with crisp pressed trousers and women in fashionable high heeled shoes walked past without noticing the woman at their feet.

The woman did not wear the face of someone who thought of social injustice or her station in life. She appeared to be whistling a tune. Clinging to her pocket was a small stuffed animal that belonged to a child, not just any child – her child. The woman on her hands and knees did her job without thinking of those who walked past her any more than they gave thought to her. She had more important things on her mind – her baby at home – the one she was working for.

To Hallie the image was an indicator that life would not always be fair or equal and that someone was always called upon to clean up the messes of someone else; that life wasn't equitable, but each individual life was profitable and had meaning. The woman on the courthouse steps found meaning in what waited for her at the end of each day and that was enough. So, Hallie worked alongside her father in the hot Indiana summers cleaning up the messes of others. With Summer's off, her father cleaned out abandoned government houses that had been foreclosed upon for various reasons. Right beside him was Hallie, picking up the messes that someone else had made

- just like the woman on the courthouse steps. Hallie wore old jeans, work gloves and the face of someone who seemed not to notice the social injustice that she would be called upon to fix a problem that a more thoughtless person had made. And like the woman on the plaque in the third drawer down, Hallie whistled or sang and found joy In life that came from a source beyond her situation.

Her grandmother had also placed a small plastic baby rattle in the drawer to represent 'stamina.' It was blue on one side and pink on the other because it did not matter whether a baby was a boy or a girl. The raising of either called for endurance. "There is nothing in life that a person is called to do that requires more stamina than to raise a baby," her grandma had told her. "They need to be fed every hour when they are born, and you won't get much sleep or rest for months and months. Remember child, the needs of the baby come first so think twice before you go down that road." Hallie heard the words as they reverberated through her mind.

Hallie sat in classes at the big red brick high school and listened to her teachers, did her studies there, and then went to work at the local I.G.A. grocery store as a clerk until closing. She did this three days each week to earn some spending money and tithe. With eyes that wanted desperately to shut and take in some much - needed sleep, Hallie pressed on with her homework until it was completed. All the while the words of her grandmother were there, telling her of how raising a baby would require more stamina than she could possibly imagine. So, the girl with the pony tail did what was required of her and thought about the seemingly impossible task of raising a baby.

It was the stack of black and white photographs bound by a red satin ribbon that held Hallie's interest more than anything else she found in that third drawer down, however. Those old photos represented something that the girl valued more than anything in life because it represented 'life' itself. It represented the life Hallie wanted for herself and never let go – it represented family. So, each night as she lay in bed, before she allowed herself to drift off to a well-deserved night of sleep, Hallie would go to the chest of drawers in the vacant attic in her mind, open the third drawer down and tenderly pull out the stack of memories contained in a 5 x 7 piece of yellowed photo paper. She mentally untied the ribbon with care because the photos were fragile and brittle. She would sort through the images of loved ones from Christmases past, birthdays, and cook – outs with runny eggs and burned fried potatoes while having Summer holidays in the park. As Hallie gently returned the old photographs to the drawer, she recalled her grandma's words once more: "The day will come dear one when people will opt to walk their dogs instead of pushing a baby stroller down the street. Babies and families will become a relic of an archaic past and an unwanted burden, cumbersome to a more modern era of progressive thinkers. Are you sure you want this – a family?" Out of a groggy sleep- filled mind Hallie would always answer with the same response – "more than anything grandma – more than anything."

It should have been obvious to anyone; it didn't take a prophet to see the "handwriting on the wall". Blake and Hallie had been a part of each other's lives since birth. It was perfectly natural to assume they would continue to be so. Their cribs had been next to each other in the church nursery. They shared the same building blocks in 'Toddler Town', and they both donned the same white smock and cap when they walked in single file across the stage as The Pastor handed out their diplomas that ushered them on to Junior High School. The Pastor coached young Blake in Little League while Hallie worked the concession stand and stayed to mow the field. But it was the Sunday evening service when they both stepped out into the center aisle and walked forward together to accept Christ as their personal Lord and Savior that applied lasting cement to the bond between the boy with the Sergeant Carter haircut and the girl with a long pony tail.

It was the content of The Pastor's topical sermon that drove the two kids into the aisle of decision. The sermon was packed full with lies and everyone knew it for what it was – *'the truth'*.

The five deadly lies that Lucifer is desperate for you to believe.

1. All Roads Lead Home.
   "…It is impossible to follow the exhortation of the bumper sticker – COEXIST. Someone is wrong. Someone has been lied to. Jesus said "I am the

way, the truth, and the life. No one comes to the Father except through me", (John 14:6) NIV - "and there's the rub."

2. "Did God really say…?"

"…fill in the blank. Whatever you want, whatever the forbidden fruit in your life – you will find an excuse for it, and you will always fall back on the oldest lie in human history in order to have it" – *"did God really say…"*

3. Life is cheap & expendable.

"…it's all about convenience and what you want at the moment and millions upon millions of lives have been lost in the carnage of keeping people happy, powerful or unencumbered."

4. God does not love you.

"…the poison of sin is so entangled into our existence that it cannot be removed; it can only be forgiven. Sin has been built into our nature from the fall of Adam and continues through you and you don't see how God can love someone in your condition. You cannot see what God sees. You can only trust Him: your eternity depends upon it."

5. Yahweh and Allah are the same.

"…Lucifer wants to be worshipped – more than anything Lucifer wants to be worshipped. (Luke

4: 1-13) He is a liar, a deceiver, and a cheat. He has deceived millions into worshiping him and he wants desperately to include you…"

The Pastor of Howard County delivered his message and it landed in the laps of Blake and Hallie like a lead weight. For Hallie, all the virtues and life values that her grandmother had left for her meant nothing if they were not grounded on the firm foundation of faith and obedience to that faith. All of her positive traits and perseverance would " give birth to the wind" as God's Word says if she remained in her seat during the benediction. For Blake, the thought of being lied to and living a life of lies himself was like battery acid on his hands as he gripped the back of the pew in front of him like a vise. They both stood up at the same time, looked each other in the eye, and knew that all their paths would be going in the same direction. Their paths may not be the yellow brick road of OZ, but they would travel it together – it was written in stone.

Approving eyes and nods from the congregation mixed with some emotional tears from parents and family members watched their crown jewels come up out of the waters of eternal life. Both kids hugged The Pastor and then they hugged each other while down in that baptistry, and they both confirmed in their hearts that they were meant to be together for as long as God provided them breath.

Fall leaves turned orange and red as the people of Howard County yearned for hot apple pie and cinnamon laced cider. Then the white snows of winter gave way to the budding of leaves of spring and dads firing up their smokers and outdoor grills as summer returned once again. Seasons change and time marches on, taking years and leaving footprints of change that can be traced in the lines on faces as challenge and life's concerns pile up. And while some things turn out different, other things remain strangely the same. Hallie's father retired from coaching, but Blake was there to take his place as the baton was handed off. To Hallie, however, the focus on sports, the long bus trips, and late Friday nights under the lights, looked just like her childhood.

Blake would arrive at the high school early to walk the halls and think. The glass trophy case took up the entire length of the foyer so the students could have something to aspire to and become – something great to accomplish with their lives. The school didn't just expose its pupils to athletic success in that trophy case. There was an abundance of success stories of students who went on to become authors, doctors, teachers, and first responders. Phil, for example, was a firefighter who saved an entire family when their Christmas tree caught fire. He saved them all but lost his own life in the process. Success can't be measured on the football field or the basketball court alone; it is measured by what is taken off the field of battle – character. Personal character is taken from the classroom and the community, as well, so the school, and Blake attempted to convey that message.

When Blake arrived at the locker room on his way to his office at the back of the gymnasium, he reviewed the clean uniforms that hung in front of each locker and the polished helmets with the big blue 'W' for the WildKats. The tile floors reflected the bright fluorescent lights that hung from the ceiling. It was his hall of gladiators. This is where he felt at home.

Hallie on the other hand added one more baby toy to an empty crib in a room that was decorated in both pink and blue. She too walked the halls, the halls of her home, looking for answers as to why her baby room remained empty and devoid of life. There was no laughter from a newborn, or dirty diapers in the pail; or crying for a bottle. The nursery was outfitted with white furniture, a new changing table, a playpen, and a beautiful new rocking chair with an afghan draped over the back just waiting to be used. Baby clothes for girls and boys hung in the closet with the price tags still on them. She had lost them both – boys and girls – six times. It did not matter how long she carried them inside her – six months, eight months or nine, the results were always the same – stillborn.

Blake and Hallie gave them names, and buried them, and Hallie visited them each day. It was the day she decided to drive home from "Baby Land" by the Church of Christ at the far end of Main Street, to visit The Pastor of Howard County – her godfather, when her life changed for the better and the hope she sought in the stack of old photographs in her grandmother's attic came true. The lights to the church were on and the doors were unlocked so Hallie let herself in and sought out The Pastor, but he was nowhere to be found. She knocked softly and entered his office. Notes from sticky pads were meticulously organized under a green bankers lamp that illuminated his desk but there was no sign of the pastor. She looked through the open window blinds and saw that the lights were on in 'the parsonage' and The Pastor's shadow could be seen in one of the rooms moving up and down with a paint roller.

The Pastor had reverently removed the picture frame that held the Kokomo "Tribune" article which told the story of Charlotte Anne and had placed it on the kitchen table for safe keeping. The girl who authored the article still attended church there and sang in the choir. She attended the pastor's Sunday School class and never missed a Wednesday evening prayer meeting. He pulled Theo's mantle from the wall so he could paint there as well, and Diver Dan looked on wonderingly with his piercing blue eyes as if wondering what on earth The Pastor was up to. Granny's gnarled old walking cane still leaned against the closet door where she had left it. No one wanted to move it – it just seemed wrong to do so. The memories had piled up and the pastor was grateful to have been involved in them, in one way or another, but the walls needed a fresh coat of paint and the carpeting needed to be cleaned so that is what he was doing when Hallie walked in the front door.

People would try to tell The Pastor of Howard County that what he saw that day was just the sun behind the girl as she came into "the parsonage," but he knew differently. "Hallie, you look absolutely radiant. Have you come to tell me you are pregnant?"

Hallie looked at The Pastor with concern in her eyes and deep suspicion at his words. "No, why would you say that" she responded. "Because you are, and the child will be perfectly fine."

"How do you know that?" she asked incredulously. "Because God just told me so. You need to go to the doctor and get a blood and pregnancy test and start taking your vitamins. Your hopes and dreams are about to come true." The man turned and went back to the task of painting but out of the corner of his eye he saw the girl with the pony tail bound down the short steps that led back to the church like a little child who had been given the most priceless gift imaginable. The look on her face told the story, and The Pastor smiled to himself while Diver Dan seemingly pondered the wisdom of telling Hallie such a thing.

Diver Dan wasn't the only one who was concerned about the news. While The Pastor had been busy painting the parsonage the unanswered phone on his desk back in the church office did not stop ringing. One very irate football coach wanted a piece of the pastor and since no one cared to pick up the phone Hallie's angry husband climbed into his pickup truck and headed out for a personal chat with The Pastor.

"What do you think you are doing telling my wife that she is pregnant. Don't you know what this will do to her?" Blake all but screamed at The Pastor as he barged into the parsonage and slammed the glass storm door behind him, leaving another very recognizable crack in the corner of the glass. "Because she is," The Pastor calmly replied to the concerned husband as he continued to roll paint on the wall.

"How could you possibly know that – you aren't a doctor! Besides, you haven't been in our bedroom!"

"Because God told me." The Pastor turned and addressed a nonplussed and very confused high school coach. "And she will be just fine and grow up to be a healthy, beautiful girl – just like her mother."

Blake was stunned. "She? It's a girl?" "Yes Blake, it's a girl." The Pastor attempted to calm a very flustered man. "But don't you get it?" Blake argued. "She has delivered still born children six times – this will kill her, and you are giving her false promises!"

"God says this child will be different because He is the one who sent it. Now go home. You have a very excited wife who needs a very supportive husband right now." And The Pastor continued to paint, and the coach continued to stare.

Hallie was, indeed, pregnant just as The Pastor had told her and a perfectly healthy little baby girl was born. The nursery of Hallie and Blake was filled with cries for bottles, with dirty diapers, and with lots and lots of smiles. The previously unused afghan became worn from months of care and love. And for the rest of Hallie's life, when she would go to bed at night, she would mentally pull out a new stack of photos from her grandma's chest of drawers. But these photographs were full of color and told a story of realized hopes and dreams fulfilled. She would remember her grandmother's words to her when she was young: *"Are you sure this is what you want child – a family?"*

"More than anything grandma – more than anything."

A young Hoosier - land coach sat next to a pregnant midwestern girl with a pony tail that was tied behind her back. They sat on a bench looking out upon the great Charles River in Boston. It was the home of legends and giants, pilgrims of their faith and founders of a nation – fighters one and all. Their child would need to be a fighter if she was to overcome the odds of her brothers and sisters back in "Baby Land." The couple had taken a road trip before the real work of life began because they believed what The Pastor had told them – what God had told them, and they wanted to wrap their minds around the task ahead. They knew the odds were against them but if God said they would be parents then they were content with the odds.

After spending a week touring Bunker Hill, the home of Paul Revere, and the many other historical sites of Boston, they decided what they would name their child – Boston. Their daughter would be named after fighters of the faith and founders of a nation.

Boston stood outside an abandoned house that sat behind a well preserved Church of Christ in Howard County. She studied the vacant building as the cottonwood was caught up in a summer wind that blew above the tall grasses swaying in the warm breeze. The massive picture window that took up most of the front porch was shattered in a million little pieces, held together by some inexplicable spell. The Pastor was gone, donut Sunday, the candy that the kids would pass out, the children's sermon; all gone. Times had indeed changed, as well as Boston herself – older now – like the abandoned 'parsonage.' She remembered still, the words her mother had taught her about the Church, The Pastor, and her great grandmother – and the chest of drawers that her mother would go to and rummage through- seeking values that could be found in the third drawer down.

Boston indeed studied the old, dilapidated house and wondered if such a chest of drawers could still be found in the world of men – or the place where her mother was told by God that she herself was coming into the world against all odds.

After long moments of reflection, she took the hands of her own son and daughter as they helped their aged mother down the sidewalk that led back to the church where 'The Pastor of Howard County' once preached – and 'The House of Spirits' silently watched them go.

Chapter Six

PAYDAY SOMEDAY

E benezer stood on hot sand in the desert sun as he looked out upon the occasional malnourished scrub brush that dotted the arid landscape. There was no breeze to cool his skin from the intense heat of the overhead sun which remained unobscured by any cloud, so sweat dripped freely from his forehead and fell off the end of his bird beak nose. A lone crow flew overhead, squawking loudly as if to laugh at him over his pitiful situation. "This must be a dream", he thought to himself. "This is the same awful crow that haunts my back yard with his incessant noise pollution." It was the only logical explanation for a crow being in the middle of that desert landscape.

He was all alone on the bluff – or so he thought. His only company other than the annoying bird above appeared to be the boulders that dotted the landscape, and reptiles that hid under the cool weight of the rocks, sheltering from the oppressive daytime heat. But as he scanned the sandy valley below him, pondering the purpose of his presence there, he heard someone call his name from behind. He turned and looked at the yawning open mouth of a rock cave. Standing in front of the opening was a handsome young man of the Middle East with the long dark curls and plain rough robes of a Hebrew nomad. The Jewish man spoke into the opening of the cave, calling out. "Ebenezer – come forth!"

Ebenezer - the observer on the bluff bore an uncanny resemblance to Scrooge from Dickens' "A Christmas Carol" - was familiar with the scene; it was the raising of Lazarus from the dead. Alone in his home he had seen it portrayed on television a hundred times at Easter or Christmas. He lived alone because no one on earth wanted anything to do with him – the most hated man in all of Howard County.

The scene before him was different than what he had seen recreated by Hollywood, however. Instead of Lazarus walking out of the tomb it was himself – Ebenezer. He appeared to be in two places at the same time. One version of himself was standing on a desert bluff as an impassioned observer, and the other Ebenezer walked out of death in answer to the Lord of life. There was no mistake. They were both indeed Ebenezer. The balding head with a ring of unkempt white hair, and his crooked nose with the pointed end that dipped toward the earth told him so, but why was he seeing this? He wasn't dead -at least not physically- so what was the meaning of this vision? And, as he mulled over in his mind the meaning of what was before him, the Hebrew turned and looked into the eyes of the sleeping man and said again – "Ebenezer come forth!"

It was the piercing blue eyes that drove the command into the soul of the hated observer, then Ebenezer woke with a start.

Ebenezer Munson lived a life of self-imposed lies and deceptions that he himself had created and lived by with religious dedication. The chief lie was his belief that he was indeed alive. He based his presupposition upon the laws of empirical nature: if a man is breathing then he is indeed alive. It may have been a recognizable law of physical nature, but it was not a true reality of the condition of spiritual man. In truth, Ebenezer Munson was as dead and decayed inside as any detestable human being could be. Another notable lie was the assumption that if others hated him it was a compliment because they must be envious of what the man possessed. Actually, Ebenezer had it backward: people hated him not because he possessed things but because things possessed him, and his insatiable lust and greed for more caused him to extract from others the blessings and hopes God himself had given them. Multitudes upon multitudes of opportunities had presented themselves to Ebenezer over the years of his hitherto ugly life to lend a helping hand to others and be a guiding light to humanity, but Ebenezer passed up every single opportunity – every single one.

If – and this was a big if – if an obituary could get someone into eternal glory and earn any credit with God, then Ebenezer Munson would be God's own go – to man. He was president of the First National Bank of Kokomo, the most notable figure in the Chamber of Commerce, 51% owner of the local steel mill and landlord to more homes in Howard County than people could count. Slumlord was more of an accurate description. Ebenezer's tenants tended to be the people who were one paycheck away from the city streets for a variety of reasons – sickness, job loss, family problems, poor life choices or simply bad luck. The wife of a bed ridden husband who was dying of brain cancer had no choice but to keep making the rent payments on time for the privilege of living in squalor, or eviction would be forthcoming. Ebenezer had a reputation, of which his tenants were well aware. Once, when the local Sheriff was forced to evict a family for back rent, the officer asked Ebenezer "just exactly how much money do you want anyway?" The children stood in the front lawn and watched as their pitiful possessions were hauled from the house and deposited in the wet morning grass of the front yard. "All of it, if I can get it," was the despicable man's stone faced response. Yes, Ebenezer was a hated man, and it was an easy thing to do because his was a reputation well earned.

Another notable lie that Ebenezer lived by was the false assumption that affluence and possessions were an indicator of God's favor. "God must love me an awful lot," Ebenezer told himself as he stood on his second - floor balcony of a grand structure of brick and stone while gazing upon the meticulously manicured lawns and fountains of a place he called home. He lived alone in a rambling mansion that was nestled into rolling acres of an estate that was securely ringed - in with black iron fences and locked gates with electronic eyes that alerted him of anyone who would come to take what belonged to him. In the three car garage sat the newest version of Cadillac. Every year he treated himself to a new car when the updated models came out – he deserved it – he was Ebenezer Munson. He owned more than anyone in Howard County. "Yes, God must love me an awful lot."

Arlene was Ebenezer's favorite tenant. She always paid her rent ten days ahead of schedule and hired a lawn care service to plant flowers, mow the yard and mulch the bushes that sat out front of her tiny duplex. She paid to have windows cleaned and the HVAC unit serviced every fall and never called her landlord for anything. She paid for everything, just like Ebenezer liked it. So, Ebenezer was saddened when he heard the news that the tenant who lived at 64 Rogers Road had passed away. But he knew it was coming. No one at her age survived pancreatic cancer. Arlene had a daughter who lived nearby and the nurses from the hospice service had kept her comfortable during her passing. Ebenezer may have loved his tenant, but it was a fondness based upon the profitability of a sound business relationship – nothing more. So, in the vein of sound business prudence, Ebenezer took out his master key and allowed himself entrance into the duplex at 64 Rogers Road just to make certain that the inside of his property was as well maintained as the outside. He didn't like surprises.

The carpeting was new – one more thing that Arlene had paid for herself - and nothing was out of place. An auburn colored chair sat in the corner next to the window to afford Arlene the light she needed to see to do her crossword puzzles and word searches that she clipped from The Kokomo "Tribune". Her eye glasses still rested on the end table next to the chair, waiting for an owner who would not return. An organ was on one wall, and an old Church hymnal propped up and opened to page 458 "Work, for the Night is Coming." (Annie L. Coghill 1836 – 1907). Ebenezer was puzzled by the old woman's interest in the song. "Surely she hasn't worked a day in over sixty years. Why the interest in work?" The landlord was clueless.

Ebenezer surveyed the value of the living room with its clean painted walls and the tidiness of the home. Protecting his financial interest was his initial driving force for visiting the place – his place - but his financial self-protection turned to suspicion. "Surely this old woman had an ulterior motive". No one Ebenezer had ever encountered looked out for his interests. It had been up to him to look out for himself. The financial wizard walked through the vacated house with grim determination to solve the riddle that he was incapable of solving. Just like the unfinished puzzles that Arlene had left on the end table. There was an answer there – he just needed to find it.

Ebenezer walked to the tiny eating area just off the simple kitchen and looked at an old oak china cabinet. Instead of beautiful and expensive cut glass dishes or antiques he would have considered valuable enough to place on demonstration he only saw cheap porcelain figurine. There were three nativity scenes of Joseph, Mary, and a young boy walking beside a donkey returning from Egypt, and The Savior carrying his own cross to his death. Ebenezer chalked it off to eccentricity and moved to the back porch where a white wooden card table held a jig saw puzzle of a Thomas Kincade picture. A simple log home looked out on a placid lake with a pair of white swans floating across the water in the full moon light. Amber – colored lights were on in the cabin and looking out of the front picture window was an elderly woman who seemed at peace and perfectly content with her simple but serene surroundings. Arlene had sat there just a week prior and envisioned herself in the chink wood log cabin of her puzzle. "I wonder if I'll have such a beautiful place to live in Heaven?" she had asked herself. Such simplicity held no value to Ebenezer though, so he moved on.

It felt unseemly to venture into the bedroom where the tenant had died, but in the interest of making certain that his investment was buttoned down, he ventured there and analyzed the room. The photo of her late husband sat on the dresser in a pewter metal frame. Her children were there as well – two boys and two girls. An extra-large set of casement windows looked out upon a pleasant back yard and private patio. Everything about the place spoke of peace – something missing from his own life. His final surprise was mounted above her headboard. A metal tree was fixed to the wall and under the roots of the tree was the phrase "The Tree of Life". Lying on the pillow sham was an envelope addressed to: "The Pastor of Howard County". Ebenezer wasn't a religious man. In fact, he could not remember the last time he was in a church. But he decided he would go to the Church of Christ at the far end of Main Street to hand deliver the deceased woman's final letter in life. He knew the Pastor and was familiar with his nick name, everyone knew him and the Church where he shepherded his flock. Ebenezer had in fact evicted at least three parishioners from his rentals.

With the letter safely tucked in his vest pocket, Ebenezer reverently let himself out and locked the door behind him. As he walked down the short sidewalk that led to his fancy black Cadillac with the expensive gold trim package, he stopped and indulged himself in one last backward look at the property and wondered who the lady really was who had lived at 64 Rogers Road. She had him stumped.

It was Sunday, so finding the pastor would be an easy task. He had never been there, but he had read about The Pastor and the church in a recent article which had appeared in the Kokomo "Tribune". The article spoke of people who had lived in the building behind the church as well – the building they referred to as 'The Parsonage'. The drive there went by quickly because his mind wasn't on the traffic or the Frisch's Big Boy restaurant with the pedestrians in the cross walk, or the Sunday talk show news program being broadcasted on the high end Delco radio in the dashboard. Ebenezer was thinking about other things: Arlene, and the figurines of Jesus and his parents, the jig saw puzzle of a humble little cabin in the woods looking out on a placid lake, and The Tree of Life mounted above the bed where Arlene had died. "Why did she have three sets of the nativity when one would do just fine?," he pondered as he scratched at his unkempt white hair. The woman evidently had lived by a unique code to which she was deeply committed, one which Ebenezer, as al those who do not know the Christ, was familiar with.

He pulled onto the fresh gravel parking lot of the country church and was annoyed at hearing the crunching sound of the gravel under his new Uniroyal tires and grimaced at the plume of dust that he had kicked up. "Now I'll have to have the car washed on the way home - they could at least pave the stupid parking lot," he groused. He did not bother to dress for a church service because Ebenezer was always dressed in perfect apparel. His black wool coat, finely pressed Johnny Carson black dress slacks and starched white Botany 500 shirt would fit in just fine he reasoned. Ebenezer was careful to park as close to the sidewalk as possible so he wouldn't scuff his new Florsheim dress shoes. He slipped quietly into the sanctuary so as not to draw attention to himself or create a need to shake someone's hand just as the music service had ended. He located a vacant pew on the back wall. He would listen to The Pastor finish his sermon, deliver the envelope and be done with it. "I don't fit in here anyway," he thought to himself.

It pleased old Ebenezer when The Pastor announced the sermon title – *'Payday Someday'*. It rang of money, and hearing about a payday pleased him greatly. But, the day's message was to take an unexpected turn on the old man.

> *"…there is a payday someday for every nation, every generation and everyone who breathes the air that God has placed in their nostrils. You will be paid back for the good or evil that you have done while you walked on God's soil – there will be a payday someday. There was a payday for Noah's generation as the flood waters swept them away just as there was a payday for Noah and his family for their faithful lives. There was a payday someday for the people of Sodom and Gomorrah for their wanton immorality and disregard for the natural laws set forth by God or to any nation or people that follow in their ill-advised path. The American Civil War was a payday someday for the idea that a mere mortal can own the soul of another man. And there will be a payday for you – and for me."*

Ebenezer sat listening to the pastor's passion and the words he spoke. To Ebenezer there seemed an element of truth to them as well. When The Pastor of Howard County got personal however, it made the old visitor on the back pew squirm in his seat. He told a story of a man he once knew who had moved to Arizona to live in a mansion of glass and steel high atop a mountain. This man's private castle looked down upon an affluent American desert town (just as the man tended to look down upon others as well). The man had everything in life that there was to have – fancy cars, a palatial home with a swimming pool that looked out upon cactus and scorpions. But the person he loved most in life was himself. The pastor's acquaintance had been a body builder and motivational speaker, and the mirror in his bedroom told him he was the greatest man in the mirage that the man called life. The similarities between the pastor's acquaintance and Ebenezer's own value system made him quite uncomfortable.

> *"...there wasn't a friend or relative that he would not betray for self-preservation, personal aggrandizement and profit and gain. He had followed the original sin of Lucifer – an insatiable lust for more. "*

The Pastor's hearers were attentive, and he laid out a compelling argument that the lust for possessions and greed were the only sins that did not leave a soil stain of guilt and shame upon a man's conscience thus enabling him to continue in his evil habit and even justify his actions in the belief that *"God must love me an awful lot – just look at what He has given to me."* Every other sin according to the pastor caused a man to feel the weight of his corrupt actions but the unquenchable thirst for more money at the expense of others too often left the conscience untouched.

> *"I will continue to pray for the primadonna in hopes of an eleventh hour conversion, but as the Apostle Paul intoned – it would be like a man entering heaven with his clothes still smoldering. It's awfully hard to be spiritually mature with only 3 minutes in the college classroom." (I Corinthians 3)*

Ebenezer continued to listen, along with everyone else, but the intended message didn't quite resonate with the old man – at least not yet.

When the sermon was finished, The Pastor of Howard County did a most unusual thing: he stood at the pulpit in total silence and scanned the audience, sitting in rapt attention as momentum built – they seemed to know what was coming and waited for it, and were eager for it. He lifted his fist into the air and shouted to his parishioners – **"Burn the Ships!"** And the audience responded with their fists raised to the heavens and shouted back in return with an enthusiasm that shook the windows – **"Burn the Ships!"**

A sense of electricity remained in the air as the people filed out of the sanctuary, giving them spiritual energy. The pianist played a song that sent chills up the spine of Ebenezer – *"Work, for the Night is Coming."* Old Ebenezer didn't believe in coincidences, but they were beginning to pile up, nonetheless.

Ebenezer was familiar with the phrase "burn the ships." The words were chiseled on the stone tablets of history and the study of history was one of the few pleasures he afforded himself. Unbeknownst to Ebenezer, the phrase meant something special to the Christian community. It was a call to leave everything behind and leave no path for retreat. Burn the past, cut all ties to the old order of things, and never look back. Soon Ebenezer would find that out as well – quite soon.

The service concluded and Ebenezer quietly and unobtrusively stepped outside and took up a position of watch under the front canopy of the church building. There he waited for the congregation to vacate the building so he could deliver Arlene's letter to The Pastor and finally go back home. He stood waiting and indulged himself by studying his expensive gold Rolex watch with the black face and cut diamond crystals set on the hour. It was a magnificent time piece, but something was missing – satisfaction. Instead of the emotion of gratification, he felt something he had never felt before - isolation. Young couples with their children filed out. Some wore a Chicago Bears jersey while others wore the colors of the Indianapolis Colts. They all bantered back and forth about the day's approaching big game, having great fun at each other's expense, and Ebenezer found himself wishing for a couple of things he had never had before - a football jersey, and a friend.

In time, The Pastor did emerge with a large ring of keys and proceeded to lock the front doors when he noticed the bystander. Ebenezer introduced himself and handed the envelope over to its addressee. The man of the cloth opened the envelope from Arlene and found a yellow sticky note which asked The Pastor to make certain Charles Munson received the letter he had in his hands.

"Is your legal name Charles Munson?" the preacher inquired. Ebenezer was perplexed. No one ever used his legal name except his banker. Ebenezer had always worn the disparaging name of a villain as a badge of honor and never attempted to make a correction. It had always pleased him to feel he was getting something over on the hateful public. "Why, yes. Why do you ask?"

"Then this letter belongs to you" The pastor meticulously folded the letter, placed it in its envelope, delivered it into the hands of its rightful owner, and departed without looking back at the totally baffled expression on the poor old man's face. Ebenezer had wasted an entire day in a church service he did not need to attend if not for the letter which he held in his hands.

Charles 'Ebenezer' Munson opened the letter and proceeded to read it aloud to himself.

"Mr. Charles Munson,

You don't know me except as one of your many tenants, but I have been praying for you for quite some time. If you are reading this then I am gone and if God has granted my final wishes, your dreams have begun. If that is the case then there will be more to come. Keep an open mind and a receptive heart for the opportunity – you won't get another.
Your faithful tenant,

Arlene"

With trembling hands, he folded the letter, placed it back in the envelope and tucked it back inside his vest pocket. It was a long road home that afternoon because Ebenezer had a lot on his mind. He picked up his favorite Chinese takeout and went into his study where he placed the plastic and cardboard containers with their strange red logo on his desk and retrieved a few of his old and tattered history books. The zeal of The Pastor and his flock as they shouted "burn the ships" would not leave his mind, so he found the familiar story of Hernando Cortez and began to read it again. Perhaps there was something he had missed.

He read again how in 1519, the Spanish explorer and conquistador sought the gold of the Aztecs. With 500 sol-diers and 100 sailors, he landed, with his 11 ships, on the pristine shores of the Yucatan. The explorer was vastly outnumbered by the native inhabitants and needed to ensure himself that his men would be motivated properly so he set fire to his own ships. This act provided his army with the incentive they needed to succeed. If the men wanted to get home again they would need to do so on enemy ships. Theirs were reduced to smoldering embers.

In his sermon, The Pastor had mentioned other points in history as well, so Ebenezer studied them also that afternoon: the world of ancient times, the decadent cities of Sodom and Gomorrah and the Great American Civil War. It was an interesting afternoon after all. The take out meal was good, as always, and the time spent studying history calmed his nerves. History was always the same, there were no surprises. Ebenezer did not like surprises. He was at peace with the world and drifted off in the comfort of his overstuffed leather chair that sat in front of the opulent white marble fireplace in his study. The clock on the mantel chimed five times - and the dreams returned.

The wind was so strong that it blew the rain like wet little pellets against his skin, stinging him like tiny little bees. Lightning flashed and arced against the backdrop of a dark and angry sky. Ebenezer could barely make out the form of a roughhewn boat made of logs and covered with pitch. Flood waters rose fast and violently, knocking the supports loose on which the huge boat rested, and the behemoth rose from the earth. Animals of every type, color and size screamed and howled from inside the ship in fear of the great noise of the ancient earth's destruction happening on just the other side of the ships wall. It all happened so fast", Ebenezer was thinking to himself. "The people had years of warning but had ignored it."

Of course Ebenezer had heard the tales of the ark of God, built by Noah and filled with the living animals of the earth but it had always seemed like a children's fairy tale. Nothing in his studies of history prepared his mind for what he was seeing in the dream. Bodies of people – young and old – male and female - and animals, were tossed in the turbulent waters and thrown against the hull of the massive ark. The constant thudding of their carcasses sickened him, and his spirit was consumed with the magnitude of the loss of earths humanity. "What were they thinking? Why did they not listen to the old preacher Noah? They had plenty of time; they just didn't take advantage of his warnings. "JUST LIKE ME!"

The inky blackness of sleep slowly receded as Ebenezer was being drawn back to his study. But there, between sleep and awake, he could still hear the muffled sound of the tumultuous waves of the ancient world while being pulled farther and farther away from them. He became aware of the tick, tick, tick of the mantle clock becoming louder and louder, alerting Ebenezer that he was in familiar territory. But he could not stay. He was being summoned to yet another destination – another dream. The last thing he heard was when the clock struck six times. An hour had passed, but the night had just begun. The strangest thing began to occur, however, before his next appointment. An abandoned chamber of his calloused old heart was being opened, and a new emotion flooded the compartment with compassion. Ebenezer was heartbroken for Noah's world. "It didn't have to be…" His thoughts trailed off in sleep once more and he was gone.

Ebenezer stood on a rocky outcropping of what appeared to have been chipped out of a mountain side. The precipice looked out upon a vast lush valley floor. The sky was a brilliant blue that belonged to a time before the pollution and smog of modern factories and automobiles. Lazy white clouds passed overhead and gave the dreamer a sense of peace. Two cities lay on the valley floor, and even though Ebenezer did not see with his own eyes what was being done within the walls of those cities, his spirit somehow knew - the unthinkable and unmentionable actions of those who lived there, in Sodom and Gomorrah.

Ebenezer saw a lone man, named Lot, holding the hand of his wife, urging her forward with haste. His two daughters trotted along, a short distance behind them, talking back and forth in a manner that resembled panic. Unmasked fear was etched upon their faces as they walked with an urgency that indicated that they were running for their lives. Ebenezer looked up into the sky above the valley floor and saw the beautiful blue sky turn a violent and angry orange and red. The colors swirled and belched out acid and flame that consumed the cities and the foliage of the entire valley. The fleeing refugees stopped in their tracks and cringed. A new emotion could be seen on their countenances – loss. All they had known was lost - the fiancés of the girls, the home and dishes of the wife, and a man's life of working and supplying for his family. Lot squeezed his wife's hand to urge her on, but she could not help herself. She looked back over her shoulder and Lot was suddenly left holding nothing but a hand of salt as it broke from the arm of she who had once been his wife. The powdery residue of salt blew in his face and stung his eyes as he wiped away tears that would not stop. The poor man had just lost the last thing he had on earth – his wife. So, the man left the pillar of salt behind – there was nothing else he could do. Lot leaned upon his two daughters for emotional support and continued walking, this time in both haste and in grief.

"Never look back Ebenezer –cut all ties and never look back", the Word spoke into the soul of the lone man on the rocky outcropping of the mountain, and he once again began gradually to hear the tick, tick, tick of the mantle clock as it chimed seven times. But the evening, and the dreaming, continued.

He had been in this place, somehow, before. He saw a bridge of three arches spanning Antietam Creek, connecting lush pastures of green field grass that swayed peacefully in the calm summer breeze. Large boulders lined the far shore and Ebenezer, could hear the birds and insects which seemed content to bide their time as the day slowly passed. The old man could have stayed there for a long time, drinking in the peace of the place, but it wasn't meant to be. The scene changed from glorious color to black and white, and the fog of acrid gunpowder and smoke from cannon and musket filled the air, choking him. Ebenezer squinted to make out the bridge – Burnside's Bridge. Ebenezer knew the battle; it was the single most deadly day of the American Civil War. Thousands upon thousands lost their lives in a war that would eventually claim 600,000 men - and boys who thought they were men. The human carnage of this war between the states would surpass that of all other American wars combined. The loss of life was staggering, and the people would never forget – or at least should not have forgotten what happens when a nation plays god.

There on Burnside's Bridge hundreds of soldiers lay dead and dying, men dressed in Union blue with brass buttons reflecting the sparking of cannon fire that filled the sky. They were stacked like cord wood and blood flowed freely as if it were cheap red wine. The life's blood of those men ran down the arches of the bridge and into the creek below which took it to faraway places. Ebenezer cried as the words of The Pastor of Howard County came back to haunt him.

...there is a payday someday for every nation, every generation and everyone who breathes the air that God has placed in their nostrils. You will be paid back for the good or evil that you have done while you walked on God's soil – there will be a payday someday. There was a payday for Noah's generation as the flood waters swept them away just as there was a payday for Noah

113

and his family for their faithful lives. There was a payday someday for the people of Sodom and Gomorrah for their wanton immorality and disregard for the natural laws set forth by God or to any nation or people that follow in their ill-advised path. The American Civil War was a payday someday for the idea that a mere mortal can own the soul of another man. And there will be a payday for you – and for me.

No quarter was requested, and no respite was offered in the battle for his soul that night, so the visions continued.

Ebenezer was deposited upon the golden shores of land of the Aztecs. The azure waters of the gulf were clear enough to see the bottom of the bay. Off in the distance sat eleven ships of war rocking back and forth in waters that seemed to mock the men and their ill – advised path. Their fate was already decided, already written in the pages of history – as is all of human history as seen by the Father above. The murmurs of anxious soldiers and sailors were audibly punctuated with apprehension. Beside Ebenezer was the Spaniard he knew to be Hernando Cortez, in his Conquistador garb and pitted iron war helmet. The man stood there looking at his ships with a live firebrand in his hands, contemplating his next move. Once he made his fateful decision the die would be cast, and his future would be sealed, as well as the future of the men who stood behind him, watching.

Long moments passed by as the stick of wood cast sparks of flame into the sky, and tensions heightened. Then the Spaniard turned to Ebenezer and held out the flaming torch and thrust it into the hands of Ebenezer wrapping both of his own hands around those of Ebenezer as he took the firebrand. Hernando Cortez looked deep into the eyes of Ebenezer with piercing blue eyes that were out of place to the Spaniard – it wasn't Cortez at all – it was the handsome young Hebrew from his earlier dream. Jesus himself looked deep into the soul of Ebenezer and with an ability to convey more than mere words – He spoke: **"burn the ships Ebenezer, burn the ships!"**

Charles 'Ebenezer' Munson woke once again, slowly, to the familiar ticking sounds of his mantle clock as it alerted the dreamer that it was midnight, and time to wake up. He had slept and dreamed long enough: it was time to act. He first fixed himself something to eat, because he was starved, and a pot of fresh coffee. The old man's mind was preoccupied with much that needed to be addressed. *"Work now, for the eternal night is coming,"* he told himself. Making some changes to his life was long overdue.

The Pastor of Howard County sat at his desk at home, looking over his schedule for the day with his own cup of morning coffee and meditating on his daily Bible readings. Arlene was on his heart, as well as the contents of the letter that she had left for Charles Munson when his cell phone rang – it was Charles Munson himself asking for an immediate meeting at the church. He seemed agitated and anxious. It was agreed upon that they would meet in The Pastor's church office within the hour. "I left the Church unlocked for the cleaning crew. Just let yourself in and I'll meet you there."

When The Pastor entered his office at the church, Charles Munson was already there, standing in the middle of the room with his fists clenching a massive amount of one hundred dollar bills. Tears streamed down his face. At the poor man's feet was a pile of bills as well. "There must be fifty thousand dollars in his fists and on the floor." The Pastor speculated.

"You have to take this," the old man choked out. "I have to get right with God."

"No," said the pastor. "You cannot buy your standing with God, Mr. Munson. I will not take your money."

Charles' Ebenezer' Munson dropped to the floor and sobbed like a desperate child. "You have to take my money. I have to make this right."

The Pastor of Howard County knelt down and draped a caring arm around the distraught old man and comforted him in his great time of repentance. "You cannot buy salvation Mr. Munson – it is a free gift given by God, not me. I cannot tell you what to do with your own money, but you cannot purchase what God has already given freely – just accept it." And there, on the floor of The Pastor of Howard County's study, in the Church of Christ at the far end of Main Street, Charles Munson's repentance was complete.

It was an incredible story of miracles and late night visitations, dreams, and harsh realities. For the remainder of his life, Charles Munson never allowed himself to be called Ebenezer again. The Pastor never knew what all was done by the old man to clean his own conscience, or what he did with his fortunes. Nor did he want to know. Mr. Charles Munson did not miss a Sunday morning service; a Sunday night prayer meeting, or a Wednesday night Bible study but his questions were always those of a curious little child. The Pastor was right: *"It's awfully hard to be spiritually mature with only 3 minutes in the college classroom."*

Mr. Munson had known of the old house behind the church building and had heard the stories of Granny and Theo. He had heard The Pastor speak of Charlotte Ann from the pulpit, and in private conversations between himself and his minister. He also knew that the little house was almost always left unlocked, so when he received his prognosis from his oncologist that his cancer was advanced and terminal, he went there – to 'The Parsonage' – to sit and think through his final movements on earth in the short time he had left. He wanted to be where others had made their journey from earth's doors to heaven's gates.

Charles Munson sat on a tufted brocade couch looking out the picture window and stole a sideways glance at the piercing blue eyes of 'Diver Dan'. The polished brass diving helmet reflected his own image that appeared to be worn, tired, and gaunt. 'Diver Dan' appeared to know how stories such as his ended. The deep – set blue eyes reminded Charles of the handsome young Hebrew of his recent dreams, and this gave him comfort. He pondered upon the reality of God's golden shores in a place called 'heaven' and wondered if the journey would cause him pain. He removed Arlene's letter from his vest pocket and read it again, reflecting on the faithful tenant from 64 Rogers Road and her intervention in his life.

In the final peaceful moments he found there – in 'The Parsonage' - Charles 'Ebenezer' Munson passed over. But the old house saw something that mere mortals could not see – the clothes of Charles were smoldering, as one who had just narrowly escaped a terrible fire. (I Corinthians 3) Charles Munson had traded a near tragic end for a beautiful new beginning.

Chapter Seven

DEAR DIARY

Dear Diary,

"I miss my father. At times it seems to me he has been gone for most of my life; other times it seems like only yesterday when we buried him in the ice crusted frozen earth in the center of town. The sleet was falling on the green burial tent where friends and family huddled under woolen blankets while we all said good – bye. I wish we had buried him in the morning instead of the afternoon: he always liked the mornings. Dad always had a habit of getting up first in the house and going outside in his boxer shorts to get the morning newspaper. He didn't know I followed him down the stairs one day and while he went outside to get his paper I shut the door behind him and locked him out. There he was - sitting on the front stoop in his boxer shorts with cars going by honking and waving and

having great fun at his expense. All the while he was hollering for me to let him back in the house. I unlocked the door and ran out the back – what fun we all had.

I surprised dad that summer morning but somehow I don't think it is possible to surprise our Father in Heaven. I spent most of my life wondering how The Garden of Eden caught God off guard and how Lucifer snuck in there and duped the poor unsuspecting naked couple. I realize now that nothing surprises our Father – He knew the whole time what would happen; it was Adam and Eve who did not know. It was a garden of life altering choices and fateful decisions. The fallen may have left the physical garden but their spiritual descendants would move back in and never leave. All of humanity would have to make the same choice – plan A (eternal life with God) or plan B (rebellion and consequences). I heard a little boy from church once say, "we are the sum total of all our decisions – it is how we are judged." I think he was right. Poor humanity: poor, poor humanity."

The cocktail of ibuprofen and aspirin was doing little to alleviate the symptoms of a rather nasty strain of flu that was coursing through the pastor's body. Chills caused him to feel cold even under a double layer of quilts. His body ached and shook just like the brittle brown leaves on the near naked trees outside his patio door while the wind blew and howled for attention. "I must have picked up someone's bug at the gym", he thought to himself in the quiet confines of his living room, and he chided himself for not being more careful. Dull black dumbbells sat on a pitted iron rack in the work – out room that invited anyone to grab them up and wrap their sweating hands around them. It was easy to pick up germs at the old Kokomo Y.M.C.A., located just off the town square. He went there daily for exercise. Thus, the virus.

There was no one there to bring him comfort in the form of chicken noodle soup so he lay on the overstuffed couch, with a blue and white cardboard box of tissues on the floor next to him along with a waste basket brimming over with used ones. Thoughts, deep thoughts, raced through his mind, the kind that come to those who devote themselves to pondering the perplexing meanings of life. But the only answers that came back to him were disquieting and clouded by fever and chills.

He was a bit old for a nose bleed but that didn't stop the blood from soaking tissue after unhelpful tissue. The pastor pulled the drenched attempt at staunching the blood flow from his nose and analyzed the failure. What he saw in his altered state of mind was something quite different than what he held in his hand. His fevered brain grew darker and his body weaker, and he drifted off in a troubled sleep.

It was a day of darkness – not light - when the once shining stars fell from the sky – the day they nailed Him to a rough and rugged tree. Cruel splinters tore into Him and sought refuge in His torn and bloody back as the mocking crown of thorns called forth a bloody trickle and life fell from his face. It was a day when evil danced in abandoned hatred and skittered across the barren landscape outside of Jerusalem in the ink of drunken success at such an evil plot and conspiracy – when creation betrayed their creator.

A solitary Roman soldier stood nearby with his battle scarred war helmet cradled in one arm while his free hand clasped the shaft of a wooden spear that dripped with the blood and water of the man who hung suspended between heaven and earth. The soldier stared and knew that his life would never be the same. "Surely He *was* the son of God!" he was heard to say.

He who was nailed to the cross was the one who hung the moon and stars in their place. He was the one who breathed on the sun and called it into being and yet at His moment of greatest need the heavens refused to shine on their creator. It was the day that creation killed its creator.

It was the day the creator killed sin. It was the day when all the poor decisions of humankind and acts of willful disobedience, were absolved. And as the vision played itself out, The Pastor of Howard County himself stood in awed silence, at the foot of the cross, while the earth shook, and his tears fell, and history was forever altered.

Dear Diary,

"I was there when the light fell – the light of men. I was there when the candle's flame sputtered and died. I was there when darkness claimed the land and the earth shook and the dead walked free. I was there when His blood ran free like a river down the tree of life and pooled on the earth that seemed unworthy to take it. Just like the tears that ran freely down my cheeks on the day that the light fell."

The Pastor of Howard County lay on his sickbed couch and thought about life's choices offered, and fateful decisions made. It was his conclusion that the essence of life was in the choosing between a variety of choices and the making of final decisions. "Decisions have genuine life altering consequences'" he thought to himself. "Those consequences cannot be altered or taken back. Life gives no mulligans." The sick pastor placed the implications of his mental process in golfing terms because it helped him to make sense of things. He would very much have preferred to be on a pleasant green golf course chasing away the local Canada geese that tried to steal his golf ball. He mulled the impact of such deep thoughts over in his mind while the fever grew worse, and his chills increased. The pastor turned on his couch like a door on its rusty hinges as the springs groaned and creaked, and the visions in his mind played out.

The golf course grass in his vision was green and lush like a thick expensive carpet. Perhaps it was his thoughts of beautiful fairways and cropped putting greens that brought the vision about, but perhaps it was something else entirely. Nothing was wild on that golf course in his mind; everything knew its own boundaries as if nature were being told what it could do and could not do. The grass was allowed to grow only so tall, and the trees kept their twigs and leaves where they belonged. Pond bottoms could be seen as if looking through expensive fine crystal and the geese drank deep at the water's edge without any fear of him, an ethereal form that was there only in spirit.

The pastor traveled at the speed of thought and intent, hovering above the beautiful land in his vision and landing at will only to take flight once more as he traveled to the four corners of the land. Valleys and forests, mountains, and grasslands; it was the same wherever he went – perfection. He finally stopped in a blaze of golden sunshine that ignited a canopy of terrarium water high above his head in a sky that moved like waves of the sea. It seemed like magic to the dreamer. Pristine shorelines of white sands looked out on an expanse of magnificent blue ocean. He knew where he was instinctively as if the dream itself told him so. No human being had been on that super-continent for millennia upon millennia. The traveler was standing on the outermost boundaries of ancient Pangea looking out upon the waters of Panthalassa – the land that was lost to man – the home of Adam and Eve before the fateful fall of humankind.

He knew the four rivers of Pangea would take him back to their headwaters in the heart of the Garden of Eden, so he traced them back to the river of life and found the two trees he sought on its banks: the tree of life and the tree of the knowledge of good and evil. The tree of life was incredible beyond words. The bark of the tree was scarlet red with veins of silver that intricately laced through the wood and wound its way skyward into its shiny silver leaves where it traded its silver color for the deep crimson of living blood which could be seen coursing through every leaf. The silver leaves with their veins of red fascinated the pastor who stared intently at their magnificent beauty. The tree was massive and cast a wide shadow where sleeping creatures lay and flowers of every color, shape and type bloomed. Nearby was the tree of good and evil. Where the tree of life was inviting and full of peace, the neighboring tree was full of intrigue and wariness. Nothing rested there and nothing grew under the cloud of its presence. The tree gave off a sense of knowledge and adventure; a sense of forbidding and invitation. The tree of the knowledge of good and evil was black as midnight and cast off no shadow. It greedily ate all the light around it and gave nothing back. The fruit of the tree was deep red and inviting however and called out in a subtle and suggestive whisper that was intoxicating to eat of it and gain its knowledge.

In his vision, The Pastor heard in the garden two distinct whispers: one whisper was full of promise and hope while the other was full of warning. And as he stood looking at the two disparate trees at the heart of the garden, he saw one lone figure approach the darkness of the tree of the knowledge of good and evil. The shadowy silhouette stood for long contemplative moments gazing at the black tree and finally stretched out his hand to partake of the forbidden fruit. In a moment of clarity, the pastor could see the youthful figure for who he was – it was Donnie – and the sleeping pastor screamed his warning in the silence of his own mind to the prodigy child of their congregation – "NO!!!!!!!!"

Five packets of artificial sweetener, one teaspoon of sugar, one heaping teaspoon of instant coffee and a splash of Hazelnut creamer; that is how Mary, the foster mother drank her morning coffee. The only difference in this daily ritual of indulgence between her and William, her husband, was that he added a splash of Italian cream to his coffee. The couple sat together in mutual silence. The covered solarium they were in was located just outside their kitchen door. They cupped mugs of the hot liquid in their hands with preoccupation and disinterest. The draw - strings of the translucent linen shades of the windows of the three season structure clanked softly together as an air conditioner blew a cool breeze that went unnoticed by the brooding couple. The sculpted outdoor carpet could be seen through the glass table top of their wrought iron patio table, revealing their slippered feet as well. They could not bring themselves to sit inside at the kitchen table, there were too many memories to be seen there – and felt. Photos encased in ornate picture frames hung with pride in every room and sat in 5 x 7 photo frames on shelves in the upper middle – class home. A white and red letter jacket hung from a hook on the hall - tree in the spacious tiled foyer - belonging jacket belonging to their adopted foster child, Donnie. The jackets hung on the hook in silence because no one was there to use it. Donnie had been missing for weeks and the unthinkable was beginning to take on unwanted shape and form in the minds of the couple who sat in their solarium seeking silence from a house that whispered in an incessant and monotonous tone that could not be silenced: "where is Donnie?" Something bad had happened to the usually dependable boy. Mary and William knew this to be true – their parental hearts told them so. Only time would unveil the elusive secret, however.

A bright eastern morning sun filtered through the shades that morning but was unable to lift the spirits of the couple. They silently sipped their coffee and looked out upon the bright blue water of the family swimming pool in the backyard. The cleaner jets moved the water while an abandoned multi – colored beach ball circled the pool in a crazy- eight pattern the cleaner jets did their job. It seemed like some harassing spirit was there taunting the foster parents that Donnie was there playing in the pool, but Donnie was not there. No one knew where he was. It had been weeks since the high school boy had boarded the school bus for a final day of classes and celebration for a graduating Senior but by the end of the day, Donnie had not come home.

William and Mary. It seemed like only a blink ago when William sat in the bleachers at a Friday night bas-ketball game with his pals. Mary walked across his field of vision; arm in arm with her fellow school girls. He would never be able to describe what Mary's girl - friends wore that evening, but he would never forget the pink cashmere sweater on Mary, or how it fit. The noise in the field house was deafening but William could still hear his heart above the din of the raucous crowd. The young man fell instantly in love with a girl who didn't even know his name yet. It was a snap decision made from a myriad of choices. It was a decision that would affect the rest of his days. It was the decision that led him to a beautiful Spring day sitting at a glass top table across from his beloved wife, Mary - and the disquiet of wondering where on earth Donnie was.

Mary could not have her own biological children. It could have been a childhood disease that caused her condition, or simply bad genes, or just the luck of the draw, but for Mary to be a mother, she would have to adopt or raise foster children. If William had been asked early on if he would have made the same decision, to wed his high school sweetheart, based upon foreknowledge, he would have said that all of life is like an old television game show. Contestants chose between door number one, door number two or door number three. No one knew what lay behind those doors. One door may have a vacation trip to Cancun while another door may reveal a used and worthless can opener. Life was very much the same in William's opinion. But In one of the sermons the couple had heard from the Pastor of Howard County, as he stood behind the wooden pulpit in the Church of Christ at the far end of Main Street, "we all live in a broken world; a broken system, and broken homes. Life is not intended to be won. It is intended to drive us to the cross of Christ. From there we will find the aid we need to navigate the rough waters of a fallen world."

Choices: life is full of them. If William and Mary chose to be parents their options were few. They could have adopted but they chose to be foster parents. It seemed to them the logical choice, one in which they could do the most good. Foster children tended to find themselves in rather difficult situations in life not of their own choosing. When they received the phone call about a two month old African American boy who had been taken from a home infested with drugs and abuse their response was automatic – "yes, we would be thrilled to take the child." That decision would lead to love during foster care, and eventually, to the commitment of adoption of Donnie.

A table sat against the wall In Willian and Mary's foyer with a single book displayed on top – it was the scrap book that catalogued the milestone events of Donnie's life. The first bite of solid food, the day his baby teeth popped through, the newspaper clippings about the Kokomo Junior High School track star, and the WildKat varsity game when Donnie scored more points individually than the entire opposition team. If one were asked to choose a single word to describe the scrap book there would be several words to choose from: love, blessing, promise and extreme potential. The milk chocolate skinned and blue eyed African could have done anything he wanted in life – anything. In the end, however, Donnie made a rather poor and fatal decision from all the choices offered to him. He chose death.

The Pastor of Howard County, revived from his bout with the flu and the influence of the medications that were fighting it, sat on his couch and watched the late Autumn sunset. It was a beautiful blend of hues – burnt orange and red and the sun exposed what few leaves remained in the trees. The sky appeared as if on fire and he took comfort that his God and Father had seen him through the past three days of sickness. Noah had the rainbow. The pastor had this setting sun all ablaze in the pronounce-ment that God was there – always there. He shuffled off to the kitchen in his stocking feet and quietly prepared a hot bowl of chicken noodle soup, placed it on a serving tray, and sat back down on the couch with his worn journal. It was a healthy way to say good – bye to the days of sick-ness that had claimed him, and eventually to his couch. He didn't know which he was the most tired of – the flu or his brown leather couch where he had taken up resi-dence for the past three days. Somewhere in the back of his mind, he made the vow – the couch would have to go, just exactly where it would go he was uncertain, just that it must go.

Dear Diary,

"Does The Father reach out and speak to His fallen world of broken people? Does God speak to us in earthquakes, famines, and pandemics? Does God speak in barely perceptible notions that enter the mind of man or the gentle nudges that touch the heart of a human soul? Yes. God is always reaching out to help and guide His people – anyone who will listen. I remember a Church sign that said, 'God speaks to us in whatever language we will hear.' I know what the sign was saying – God will do whatever it takes to get us to pay attention and listen to Him. It may be in poverty, or it may be in times of blessing. It may be the loss of a loved one or the birth of a child. Seldom does God reach out in an audible voice that the Holy Spirit imprints upon our understanding, so if He does – we should be very careful to pay attention. That is why I pray for Donnie. I perceive that he is in the midst of a time of testing."

The Pastor laid his journal down and picked up his evening dinner tray and moved to the kitchen with his empty bowl when the motion detectors in his yard kicked on and activated a bank of flood lamps that lit up the front yard. The sun had set, and darkness had once again claimed the land. The Pastor set the tray by the sink; he would come back to clean up later. The activity in his front yard was of more immediate concern. The gravel driveway glistened as the flood lamps reflected off the fresh limestone powder and rocks. A gentle evening breeze played with what few leaves remained on the row of maple trees which lined the driveway. Nothing seemed out of the ordinary but as The Pastor reached out to turn off the motion sensors, he noticed something sticking out from under his pickup. A pair of dirty red tennis shoes was attached to a ragged pair of jeans. Someone was under his truck.

The man who made his living with words was confident that regardless of whoever was under his truck, he would be able to talk his way clear of any potential danger. So, he ventured out the screen door and down the concrete steps, armed only with a flashlight in hand to see who was making an encampment under the protection of his F-150. He was the dirtiest person The Pastor had ever seen. Dirt, grease, and grime were smeared into his hair and on his face. It was impossible to determine any identity, but gender was more obvious; the vagabond was clearly a young man, and probably an athlete. Lean corded arms and muscular legs amply filled out jeans that were as dirty as the man's face but when the beam of the pastors flashlight reflected off a Senior class ring to Kokomo High, The Pastor of Howard County knew immediately who he was looking at: it was Donnie.

The Pastor tried everything he could think of to rouse the incoherent lad, but the youth could not come out of his drug induced stupor. The preacher gave up and simply grabbed the boy by his red suede Converse Allstars and dragged him and his muddy shoes out from under the pickup and onto the damp evening grass of the front yard. The beam from the flashlight revealed Donnie's dilated pupils. His overdosed state was obvious and heartbreaking. Donnie was higher than a kite.

The Pastor picked up Donnie fireman – style and carried him into the house. He stripped the filthy clothes from the boy and stood with him in the shower, under freezing cold water. The Pastor was the support for Donnie at that time when Donnie could not stand there alone. William and Mary had stood with Donnie when the two - month old baby could not stand on his own. The Church stood with Donnie and parishioners filled the stands, to watch their prodigy child defeat the opposition at every sporting event. In the end though, Donnie would need to stand alone just as all people must. Everyone eventually stands alone to answer for their decisions they have made in life – it's what defines.

The Pastor was miserable standing in the ice cold water with Donnie. His teeth chattered and his body shook – he was so cold. Donnie could barely notice the cold water running down his body because of his condition but eventually began to come back to earth - much to the relief of the man who was trying desperately to bring him back into the realm of the living. After a pot of hot black coffee, some much needed nutritious food, and the retrieval of his once soiled clothing, but now washed, Donnie told The Pastor of his past few weeks after joining a local street gang. The drugs and initiations were a bleary fog that only hinted at the activities of the days since his last day of high school. Donnie missed his graduation and all the accolades from his classmates and an admiring faculty and staff. All his graduation presents remained on his bed at home – unopened. The head baseball coach from Stanford had been at graduation to see his greatest new prospect in over a decade but Donnie was not there. It was like a rerun of *'It's a Wonderful Life'* but Donnie didn't see the holes he had left in the events of life since he was gone, only the people left behind could see the void.

Donnie had walked through the triple stone arches of Klein Field at Sunken Diamond in Stanford, California just weeks earlier while on Spring break. The campus reminded him of an old Catholic monastery settled among rolling California hills located behind the school. Green grasses and a brilliant blue sky that reached up and touched the heavens felt like an oasis of promise and hope for a minority living in rural Indiana. Donnie loved the school logo of a solitary capitol red letter 'S' with the lone green pine tree. From a distance it looked to him like the number one – and that is how his future felt. Donnie felt like he was number one but in the end he traded it all for a dirty needle and a restaurant's greasy food dumpster in an alley in downtown Indianapolis until he made his way to the pastor's house under the cover of darkness. It wasn't a good trade, and gangs are difficult to run from; once you're in – you're in.

Donnie arrived late to classes at Stanford that fall. The Church sent money, so he didn't have to work and so did William and Mary naturally. The boy thrived in the California sun and when baseball season kicked off so did Donnie. The coach and the University knew they had made the right choice when they recruited Donnie. "Sports Illustrated" did a write up on the golden boy from central Indiana and how Stanford recruited the brightest college prospect away from the Indiana Hoosiers. The sports magazine didn't intend to, but they had drawn a large red target on Donnie's back. If the boy with gossamer wings had moved to the land of gold to sell real estate or perhaps work in silicon valley no one would have noticed, but a gang in Indianapolis saw the magazine article about the local sports hero, and like a pack of rabid wolves, they followed the road map to Donnie. After all, when it comes to gang life, once you're in – you're in.

It was a lapse of judgement on Donnie's part when he stretched out his arm to take a single bite of a forbidden fruit. Just one bite, that's all it took, and his life on earth was as good as over. Much like when God told Adam and Eve not to eat the fruit of the tree of the knowledge of good and evil or "you will surely die." Adam and Eve did not die that day, but the process of death did indeed begin. So too with Donnie, he did not die under the truck of his spiritual mentor but like so many poor decisions made by man, death did eventually come as a result of his actions.

The body of the promising recruit of Stanford University was found on top of home plate at the 'Sunken Diamond' at the end of an amazing baseball season. He had been stripped down to his briefs and the myriad of syringes sticking out of his body made him look like a human pin cushion. Small trickles of blood oozed from each puncture wound as a warning to anyone who dared to depart from gang life, no matter how far away one tried to escape. William and Mary never saw the crime scene photos of their dear little two – month old boy, the track star, the high school athlete, the church favorite, but their pastor did, when he flew out and met with the Stanford City Police to claim the body for burial on behalf of heart-broken parents too numb to make the long flight. It was just one more mental image given to a lifelong minister of God that left a permanent impression behind – or more accurately a scar if the pastor were asked to describe it.

The funeral for Donnie took place on a beautiful spring day in central Indiana when the tulip trees were in full bloom and the Wabash River still ran full from the winter snows. The Church of Christ at the far end of Main Street was packed with members of the congregation and students and teachers from Kokomo High School. Even the head baseball coach from Indiana University in Bloomington attended. Donnie belonged to all of the

Hoosier state, so it didn't surprise anyone at the size of the crowd or its diversity. A beautiful young girl that had attended high school with Donnie sang a placid and hypnotic rendition of a popular song of the day – *'Isn't Life Strange'*. (Moody Blues, Seventh Sojourn) © 1972. No one knew that she secretly loved him, but it came as no surprise since everyone there did.

The eulogy, naturally, was delivered by the Pastor of Howard County, the mentor and protégé of so many in attendance. It was a message that remained long in the minds of many who attended there that day, until the time of their own passing. The obituary clippings for Donnie taken from the Kokomo "Tribune" would all turn yellow and brittle over time, but the words of the pastor that day would not.

"What is it that defines a life lived? Is it the failures of a man that tells us who he was or how much his life was worth? Was it the successes of his existence that determines the justification for his breath? Is there a mathematical calculation that deducts the debits from the credits and lifts the scales of judgement in our favor? If a man can be saved at the eleventh hour and one fateful decision erase all past misdeeds, can a single poor decision at the eleventh hour erase an entire lifetime of walking with God? Is God bound by how we perceive time and the course of the human events of our lives and where those events take place? Yes - and - no.

...and the baby cried. A ruddy skinned boy covered with thick black hair cried as his mother laid him down. He seemed just another child born into the fallen world of men, but God hated the child even before the infant was born. How could it be that God of the universe and all created things bore such emotion toward a soul who hadn't even made a single self – willed choice in life? Perhaps our creator is not bound by the chronological ordering of things as humans are. Perhaps God saw the soil of Esau's soul and already knew the outcome of the man and his future lineage. Perhaps God can jump to the end of our story and read the book of our lives that we ourselves haven't even written yet. Perhaps the judgements of God are not as dependent upon the process of time as we think.

Perhaps our God and creator looks upon the soil of the soul of Donnie and the years of walking with him and doesn't see the boy who made an eleventh hour decision that had terrible consequences. I can't bring myself to conclude that God would dismiss so lightly the faithful years of Donnie's life – the care he had for our youth group, the time spent working with the boys at basketball and tossing the baseball...

In my mind's eye, I am still going for an evening run with Donnie. When I look over and see the sun in his eyes and his playful smile as we talk and run together. We both knew he could be miles ahead of me – his talent was so much superior to mine. In my mind's eye, I see Jesus going for an evening run with Donnie, too. When Donnie looks over and sees the sun in the Savior's eyes and his playful smile as they talk and run together. Jesus could be miles ahead of him – his talent so much superior…

Perhaps our God is bigger than you might think…"

The children of the Church of Christ's youth group had all but ruined the upholstery of the existing sofa that sat in the parsonage. With no current occupant, the kids had conducted their Sunday evening gatherings there and the couch was the recipient of a multitude of cola spills, pizza stains and mud streaks from dirty little tennis shoes. "All good," thought the pastor. "I'll replace it with that leather couch of mine. I was looking for a place to unload it anyway. Let's see the little mud hens ruin that tough skinned old bird."

So, as the Hoosier sun was setting and casting its brilliant final rays over just another ordinary day through the picture window of the old parsonage, Diver Dan looked down from his perch on the hand carved wood mantle mounted to the wall across from The Pastor's old sofa and saw something that humans could not. Metal skin and blue LED lights for eyes saw the emotions and visions and dreams radiate from the brown leather couch like heat waves off a concrete sidewalk in the middle of August. Layer upon layer of possibilities rose up from it like different tracks playing from an old DVD. The Pastor had so permeated the article of furniture with his own thoughts while suffering from sickness that they had become an inseparable part of it.

The potential of a timeline played out as The Pastor had moved through his life alone without the companionship of a spouse. His friend, lover, and wife had died so many years prior, but a different path played itself out before the eyes of Diver Dan as he watched the variant time lines play out before him. A different wife; the product of a different decision made from a different set of options moved with grace and dignity in a kitchen that was familiar to the pastor – but the woman was not.

Another track played itself out where Donnie arrived home for Christmas break from Stanford during his Senior year at the University. A giant white flocked Christmas tree with black and white gingham bows and silver balls sat tall and erect in the massive foyer where a scrap book proudly sat with clippings of all the collegiate successes of the golden boy that made all the right decisions in life. William and Mary were told of their son's decision to play baseball for the Chicago Cubs – something that would make his preacher ecstatic and Donnie couldn't wait to tell him personally. What might the lives and hearts of William and Mary been like had such a potential time line become their own reality – unfortunately, they would never know.

Track after potential track played out before a dispassionate, man – made inanimate object but the possibilities were real just the same. The decisions were real; they were just different. The players were the same, but the time lines were altered so as to accommodate a different set of decisions and a different set of outcomes. After all, a dispassionate, man – made inanimate object can see things that flesh, and blood cannot.

The Pastor would very much have wanted to witness the final track that played itself out, there in the unoccupied parsonage that evening. A stunningly beautiful fair skinned woman with long shining dark hair stood looking at a massively tall tree with black leaves talking to a serpent. She listened ever so intently, said something to the talking creature and simply walked away. She did not reach out her hand to partake of the tempting forbidden fruit. She did not discuss the issue any further with the serpent. She did not evaluate the accuracy of his subtle lies or the potential merits of what she was being offered. She simply walked away.

Diver Dan had simply used the emotions that The Pastor had infused into the couch as a roadmap for potential alternate timelines, and how if a different set of decisions had been made from the same set of choices offered, it would have resulted in something altogether different than what had ultimately transpired.

The Church buried Donnie on a fair spring day in the same graveyard where The Pastor's father lay. It was the same graveyard where Granny and Theo had been laid to rest, along with so many other cherished people whom he had grown to love but grudgingly dismissed from the yellowing brittle pages of his life. It had begun to seem like a dangerous game of dodgeball to the small town preacher. At times he felt like the last man standing in a vacant field. He had been pastor to so many people over the years. So many were now gone to him.

In an effort to clear his mind and start over, The Pastor of Howard County sat alone in a local coffee shop with a cup of hot black coffee on his table; nothing fancy for him, just plain black coffee. He sat and sipped while looking out through the multiple plate glass windows and noticed how many handprints and finger smudges had accumulated on the glass. He looked through the glass at the traffic as it passed by in a continuous speedy effort to arrive at some important destination, but his vision always came back to the fingerprints on the glass. The pastor took up his leather bound journal and the only frivolous possession he owned, a classic black fountain pen, and began to write.

Dear Diary,

Ponderings...

"What if *time itself were like a plate glass window? Since glass is neither a solid nor a liquid but rather an amorphous solid somewhere between the two, and since glass never completely stops moving yet can be measured – perhaps time is a lot like glass. Perhaps one reason God never told anyone the final day that the world will end is because with God time is somewhat fluid. His business and no one else's'.*

What if *human life is very much like a finger print on a two dimensional pane of glass? We can only see those smudges closest to us but God on the other hand can see them all. What if the cross of Christ shows crimson red and the blood of His cross runs throughout all of time like veins that touch one print and then another that turns them red – our stamp?*

Is it possible that there are other panes of glass comprised of fingerprints made by people who are not broken and do not live in a broken world such as mine? Is it possible that on a different timeline there never was a fall?

What if *God foreknew what He would do in Genesis 3:15 to rectify the fall but Jesus didn't know the day or hour of his return because He wasn't taken from the essence of God until His incarnation. What if the sacrifice of Jesus wasn't an event in time but rather eternity. Perhaps God sacrificed more than what we can comprehend.*

What if..."

Chapter Eight

GRADUATION DAY:
THE FUTURE AWAITS

An *ordinary* high school boy approaches a wall of tempered glass and a matching pair of heavy glass doors. These doors lead to his *extraordinary* future – a future that patiently waits to be discovered. He has come and gone through those doors for four long monotonous years of education - never wanting to be there really; it was just a requirement that he do so – part of a system of hoops that most people pass through. The cavernous school foyer and massive cafeteria were near, but he does not need to turn around to see them. They will be indelibly imprinted upon his mind. The clamor of excitable teenagers will always be there when he thinks of that building. Tan cinder block walls and polished tile floors reflect the bright fluorescent lights that are on his side of those double doors, but the future however, lay on the other side of them. It is graduation day at Kokomo High, and the uncharted waters of a foreign land lie ahead;

a realm of fresh decisions and choices of self – will, where his destiny is his own. For the first time in his hitherto short life he is genuinely both frightened and excited, all at the same time.

It was graduation season once again and The Pastor of Howard County remembered what it was like for him to graduate from high school and how the future had frightened him. He felt different when he graduated from seminary though. He had purpose then. He had a calling. But now he was wondering about all the kids who were about to set their feet on their life – journey. "I wonder if it would frighten them even more if they knew where the road would take them?" The pastor pondered.

It was the month of May, when high school and university students across the nation marched in single file across the carpeted stages of auditoriums and hardwood floors of gymnasiums for their hard – earned diplomas. Students were being ushered into their own futures. To the ordinary citizens who lived near the Indiana University campus in Bloomington, the month of May was when Christmas seemed to come early. The sorority and frat houses along 3rd Street and 10th Street and Jordan Avenue now sat empty, but those who had recently occupied those dwellings had taken part in the annual ritual of leaving behind many of their prized possessions on the front lawns, sidewalks, tree plots and medians along Greek Row. Television sets, mini – bar refrigerators, couches and even articles of expensive clothing were strewn about, screaming "take me – I'm yours!" Parents of the students had bought the stuff, so kids didn't have anything invested in the leaving of it. But a grateful parade of rust eaten, red – neck pick - up trucks were grateful to fly the red and white candy - cane colored flags of I.U. from their antennas on the day they gathered the loot. Locals thought it was the grandest thing imaginable. To onlookers, it looked like the *'Grapes of Wrath'* coming out of the college neighborhoods all loaded down with tangible evidence that you really could get something for nothing. The only thing missing was granny on top of the loot with her moonshine bottle, and she could probably have been spotted in the ragtag procession if someone had taken time to look.

As this and other activities marking the end of the academic year were winding down outside, The Pastor of Howard County stood in front of a motel bathroom mirror. He adjusted his plain black tie and examined his starched white shirt while reflecting on what it had felt like for him, years ago, to have an undeclared future and a clean slate on which to write his own story. The shocks of gray that once ran through his hair had now turned white, claiming more real estate on his head than the last time he had genuinely studied his reflection. The widow's peak of his hair line had receded even farther, and his once - rugged shoulders had a more pronounced stoop to them. Time was claiming what time always claimed and he could do nothing but watch.

Nostalgia caused him to reflect back many decades in his own past to the eight - track player in the wood – grain dashboard of his father's old Oldsmobile as a teen – age boy, and how his dad would listen to a certain song that spoke about the September years of a man's life. The pastor had unwittingly walked into his own September years when the green summer leaves of youth turn orange, with tips of red. The heat of his summer days had turned to a sharp chill wind from the north, but the hope of an unknown future would be presented to a graduating class of Indiana University students that after-noon and the pastor had made the trip from the central Indiana cornfields to Bloomington to show his support for Jamie, one of many happy surprises to come out of the pastor's Church of Christ, down at the far end of Main Street in Kokomo.

The pastor turned from the mirror, sat down on the edge of his motel room bed, and contemplated again the concept of 'time'. He had done a lot of that during his ministry – contemplation about time. He had seen con-stant change in the world during his tenure as preacher and caregiver to an entire county of people. Some of those changes had been good, while some of them had not been. Perhaps it was because he was in a major college town with a strong athletic and music program that drove his thinking. At that moment he was inclined to picture time as a fancy marching band, perhaps the well – known IU

Marching Hundred. He could visualize colorful red and white uniforms, sparkling silver flutes, braided snare drums and polished trombones reflecting the sun's rays. In his imagination, confetti would fly in the air as the band marched past the throngs of people who cheered and clapped their hands as the festive music played. He visualized the confetti as delicate memories strewn here and there on the pathway of life, sidewalks, and even caught up in the ladies hair – but there was one thing that time always leaves behind: time is always taking but in its wake, it leaves memories.

The Pastor picked up one of those little pieces of confetti in his mind and held it between his index finger and thumb. He rolled it around so he could look at it from both sides and recognized it as the memory of Jamie, Amanda and their two parents. He recalled the naughty little boy that Jamie had once been, and his brown - eyed sister with the Shirly Temple hair. They had grown up in the parsonage behind the Church because their family had nowhere else to go. He further remembered what had happened while they lived there in the humble little parsonage – what had happened to them all.

The pastor had seen it all during his ministry; at least it seemed to him to be so. He had visited families of his congregation and had seen loving, caring fathers playing catch with a new baseball and new gloves for the dad and his boy. He had been invited to family cookouts with burned hamburgers and scorched hot dogs, and everybody just laughed and had fun eating the blackened food. It made for fun memories. Jamie didn't have any of that as a boy and it broke the pastor's heart when he reflected back upon the childhood of Jamie.

The marching band of time had strewn some rather unattractive confetti memories down the life - path of Jamie, but when he reflected back upon his short time at the parsonage, they were the only memories about his upbringing that he cherished. So many of those good memories were because of the church's youth group, the parsonage, and The Pastor of Howard County.

Jamie had felt a deep compassion for Amanda, his sister, and his precious mother, but he had vowed to leave behind the diseased memories of his father. So, after graduating from Kokomo High, he needed to get away from the cornfields of north central Indiana. Somehow he found a way to sort through the brown and molded memories and keep the pretty pastel ones of his youth and to create new ones going forward. He chose to do his sorting out as a college student downstate, on the Indiana University campus.

Jamie had been a walking tornado as a child, before meeting The Pastor and The Savior he preached about. Holes in bedroom walls from angry little balled - up fists, shattered windows from baseball bats, and kitchen steak knives driven deep into the sidewalls of his father's all terrain truck tires all screamed of a shattered spirit and broken heart. Jamie's mother and school counselor both looked for a cause, something that might have come with a long Latin name – something that could be treated with pills and therapy. The Pastor of Howard County, however, saw things for what they were – abject resentment and hatred for an abusive drunk and hate - filled father.

Their story wasn't unfamiliar in a broken world where broken people tried to walk down life's pathways together. The story of Jamie and Amanda's parents was an all too common story as seen by the Father above. A handsome young man fell in love and married a beautiful girl with sandy colored hair and olive skin that had the warmth of the sun seemingly baked in. The freckles on her nose crinkled when she squinted, and the corners of her mouth showed how easy it was for her to laugh. Everything seemed roses until the babies arrived (Jamie and Amanda) with their constant crying and demands for formula and diapers that eventually turned into worn out sneakers and holes in jeans. Sleep deprivation, overdue bills and phone calls from debt collectors tested the stressed parent's convictions and determination. That's when the voices started in the father's head. That's when the poison of resentment replaced youth's love and passion. That's when the drinking began – it's when the beatings began.

For Jamie and Amanda's harried father, every work day began in the same manner – coffee and a donut at the local convenience store before the long drive north to Lafayette, Indiana to pretend to be something he was not – a polished car salesman for a reputable high end auto dealership. He drove an old vintage pick - up truck, which seemed to underscore the undeniable truth that he would never be financially capable of buying what he sold. Every single signed contract with a newly satisfied customer told him he was living a lie; that he was worthless; that his end in life would be just as dismal as each passing day. Every drive back home ended in the same manner as well, which involved a brown paper bag with a hidden glass bottle inside it, and more beatings doled out to his wife and children. The family dog eventually became tired of it and ran away – something the kids could not do.

The Pastor of Howard County and his congregation offered the turning point for the little family when their world hit a block wall, and the parsonage provided a safe haven in which to live. Junior high school came and went for both children as did high school. Four additional years of college then passed after Jamie had loaded up his Jeep and headed out to Indiana University. He left the parsonage the day after his high school graduation ceremony, so he could get a jump on finding a job before the bulk of students arrived in Bloomington for fall semester. He just trusted that Amanda and his mom would be okay – something that didn't quite pan out as hoped. When things fell apart, they did so in a big way. After all, It had seemed like a reasonable length of time since his father had lapsed into a drunken and violent outburst – since they were both young teens actually – when they were forced to take refuge in "the parsonage" behind the Church of Christ at the far end of Main Street. So, he had left Amanda alone with their parents to finish her Senior year at Kokomo High School and went off to I.U. She was strong and independent and had her own friends and social circles. Amanda didn't need her slightly older brother anymore, or at least that was what his loving sister wanted Jamie to think – and he did. So, he wasn't there for his sister on the night she needed him most – but their pastor was.

When Jamie had arrived on campus for the first time he wanted to see the sights of Bloomington and the campus, so he mounted his orange and black ten - speed bike with the off road knobby tires because he chose to see the town and the campus up close and personal. He could have taken his Jeep Renegade with the snap off canvas top around town, but he wanted to feel the open air, hear every sound above the roar of a man - made engine, and smell the smells of the town without having to look through a glass windshield. It was a beautiful sunny fall day, perfect for riding outdoors, and just cool enough for the local restaurants to have their doors standing wide open to the crowds of young customers huddled together on the eatery patios and fenced - in verandas. Smells from the Pizzeria near the campus on Kirkwood Avenue wafted through the air as an open invitation to spend time there. He peddled past Nick's English Hut where he and his pals would typically congregate after a crazy Fall football Saturday and Ladyman's Diner where he would eventually take his dates on special occasions.

Jamie had done his homework prior to arriving in Bloomington. His pastor had told him about his own grandfather's wholesale grocery warehouse downtown on East 3rd street – The Roy Burns Wholesale. He rode past there to see what was left of the old building. The Monon railroad once had a rail spur there where sugar, flour and canned goods were unloaded by hand by rugged and hard working men; men made tough by the war years and the Korean Conflict. They were part of a generation that knew so little about peace. The tracks had all been removed, and where railroad cars once traveled, countless people walked along a paved path seeking a modicum of peaceful meditation and health in an age that afforded such an elusive thing.

Jamie peddled his ten – speed down the geographical barrier along Indiana and Kirkwood Avenues that constituted an invisible boundary between the campus and the town. It was said that a famous I.U. alumnus had proposed building arched gates leading to the campus, at the Far East end of Kirkwood Avenue, in memory of his parents. Jamie visualized the Arc d'Triumphe in Paris standing there, demanding attention, notifying new scholars they were entering a sacred place of learning, a place where chasing dreams counted as something special. For Jamie it was something more than that though, it was a place where the bad dreams of life could be laid to rest and forgotten, one piece of brown confetti at a time.

He peddled north a few blocks and stopped his bike on the sidewalk to gaze at a tired red brick building with greying limestone steps that had once been a Church of Christ there on Indiana Avenue. The beautiful stained glass windows were still there, but the seekers of truth were all gone, consumed by the marching band of time. The church had been sold like so many other buildings of worship in an era that was slowly forgetting its heritage, like an Alzheimer's patient who loses one piece of precious memory at a time.

Jamie would do his own forgetting but unlike the unfortunate onset of an Alzheimer's patient, Jamie's loss of memory was purposeful and intentional. It was a necessary part of healing. He chose to do most of his forgetting on the hiking trails of the Charles C. Deam Wilderness and the banks of the placid waters of Lake Monroe just south of Bloomington. He would go there on weekends in his faithful Jeep as his college schedule allowed. It was his own special place of peace. It was the place where he buried his father.

Jamie had spent his childhood lashing out at tangible inanimate objects, like walls made of gypsum, and glass windows that could not fight back – anything he could find to destroy in order to emotionally and financially complicate the life of his father- both emotionally and financially. Amanda, however, simply withdrew deep into herself, with a hatred for the evil she saw and felt from her father. She sought for the resolution of violence done to her in the annals of warfare and the battlefields of history, where evil men were destroyed with bullets, tanks and flying aircraft that dropped bombs on ammunition plants behind enemy lines. She withdrew into the battlefields of history where evil could legitimately be destroyed by good. She read about ridding the world of bullies on the stage of open and declared war until she would eventually stand on that stage of war herself and push back against the ever encroaching darkness of hate, prejudice and evil.

In her mind's eye as she read book after book of human kind's attempt to fight back, she pictured herself at Devil's Den fighting alongside with Dan C. Sickles at Gettysburg before the fateful frontal attack of 'Pickett's Charge' and the wholesale slaughter of so many men that happened there on a hot Pennsylvania Summer day in 1863. She was there standing her ground on Burnside's bridge at the national disaster of Antietam Creek. In her mind, she was the one who set the mine charges at Petersburg during the 'Battle of the Crater' when the American Civil War was grinding to a halt.

Amanda felt that anyone with half a soul should have seen the sin of slavery for what it was, and the spiritual lunacy of calling upon the God who created all men in *His* image to come to the aid of those who sought to enslave the souls of men and exploit them just because they could. It was incomprehensible to her why any human would need to think through what should have been common sense – if not spiritually then with all decent human emotion and compassion.

In her mind, she was also there when the earth movers pushed the mountains of dead corpses of Auschwitz and Dachau into open trenches of mass graves and swore in her soul that she was going to rid the world of as many ruthless, heartless cruel men as she could sniff out; *men like her father*, and she did exactly that.

Jamie had enrolled as a freshman at Indiana University in Bloomington the year before Amanda graduated from High School believing his sister would be alright. She knew it was the right thing for him to do. Her brother needed to get away and find his own path. Amanda had put on a convincing act that she didn't need Jamie anymore; that she was independent and self-confident. It was painful for her to do so but Jamie never would have left otherwise.

It was the events that took place the night before her own high school graduation that set Amanda's future in motion. It was the fateful night when evil sought to destroy her, but which only succeeded in steeling her own resolve to go through with what she knew in her own heart needed to be done. It was the night when her own father tied her to a chair and hung her from the Wildcat Creek Bridge to teach her a lesson she did not deserve. It was the night she drove herself to the recruiting office in Kokomo and enlisted in the United States Army. In her own way, she was going to kill her father.

Just exactly why the pretty young wife and mother of two helpless children chose to remain in such a tempest of violence and bodily harm was anyone's guess. It was a mystery to all who knew the details about the situation – and most people in the small town did know. Plenty of opinions about it were openly discussed over various dinner tables on any given evening. Newspaper articles concerning the frequent wail of sirens coming from a police cruiser and or an emergency paramedic van speeding to the Saint Joseph Emergency Room would appear in the Kokomo "Tribune". Neighbors didn't need to be gossips to know there was a problem in Howard County. News of it was delivered to each and every household doorstep, every single morning in the local newspaper.

Perhaps the reason Jamie and Amada's mother stuck around was loyalty to her children, or stubborn pride, or an unwillingness to admit personal defeat that kept the young mother frozen in place. Maybe it was an unreasonable fear of the unknown that blocked her resolve to escape her situation. The Pastor had his own opinions about why the woman could not pull the trigger on a decision that appeared all but black and white, but his counsel had not been sought – yet.

A song would play over and over in the woman's heart and mind. It was a familiar song she had heard her own mother sing to herself repetitiously as she ironed her husband's shirts and prepared his meals. The tune compared the soul of man to a heart of fragile glass and how the Savior can mend the shattered pieces and make it whole again. It was imperative to have faith that her faithful friend could and would heal her own husbands' heart of broken glass. The song was remembered and kept in a secret space in the heart and mind of an abused young wife and mother of two frightened and damaged children. It was a hymn that played on an endless loop of hope – it had to be true – it was true for her own mother and father, so it had to be true for her and her husband – it just had to.

The local landlords didn't know the song though; they could not hear the refrain of hope and promise that the young wife and mother clung to out of desperation. So, one by one, the family of four was evicted from rented houses with broken glass and holes in walls, while a mother prayed with deep emotion to God for guidance over those turbulent waters. It came to her that there was a Church in town that had made it their mission to help the helpless and to supply the needs of the needy, so she went to The Pastor of Howard County. She asked him if her small family could take up residence in the little parsonage with the big picture window overlooking the front porch. Looking out that window, she could take consolation from the warm blaze of Hoosier sunsets.

Diver Dan sat atop his perch on the ornately carved mantle and watched with his bright blue eyes as the family came and went - in and out of the front Hobbit door with their personal affects. He could see with dispassionate eyes the heavy burdens they carried in addition to their few tattered possessions. He saw the soil of fear and hurt upon the spirit - worn boy and his sister with the Shirley Temple hair and pretty brown eyes. He saw the smoke of desperation that clung like a thick gray cloud to the mother, and the sinister presence of dark, demonic, oppression like so many coiled up serpents coiling around and shrouding the defeated father and husband.

Wayne and the board of elders knew what they were in for – they could read the Kokomo "Tribune" - just as well as anyone in town. So, they made it mandatory that the entire family of four participate in counseling under The Pastor as a condition of their presence in the parsonage. Wayne knew they could not mandate that the family attend church services, however. That would violate their self- will which God in His own wisdom bestows on all His creation. Besides, it would not accomplish what was needed, but they did make their desires known to that affect. But the mother and her two children did attend faithfully, of their own volition, while the husband remained at home to watch the NFL Sunday game of the week with a six – pack of locally brewed ale from one of the hip taverns and a slice or two of brick oven pizza.

It appeared to be an ordinary Sunday the day Jamie, Amanda and their mother walked in late for church services. The vibrations of the grand pipe organ were still in the air as The Pastor took his place behind the pulpit and began to deliver his sermon. It wasn't a long walk from the parsonage to the doors of the church building and the weather was fine, but to this beleaguered wife and mother it was like battling against a strong hurricane wind that pushed against her as she took each tentative step. It was as if her old and scuffed dress shoes were stuck in the mud and each struggling step pulled at her feet with a sucking sound that made her feel she was being held in place.

> *"God does not want your cast offs; He deserves more respect than that. God does not want your best; He does not share. God does not want part of you, He wants all of you. "*

The sermon was about Hannah, a mother who had given everything – her dreams, and all she ever wanted in life - and her only child as well. It was a familiar message, really, – such as a Father who gave His one and only begotten son.

It was a simple message of faith the pastor laid out that Sunday morning – Christianity 101. It was basic understanding to most of the congregation and their complacent body language that morning told the pastor so. But, to a mother of two on the back row it was radical thinking, as alien as if she had just heard from the pulpit about a UFO. Her children were all she had in the world. The thought of giving them over to God completely and unequivocally, to do with as He deemed best, frightened her even more than any beating her husband could dole out. Her walls of resistance slowly crumbled, however, as she absorbed the words of The Pastor, and a quiet spirit of submission fell upon her. She felt something she had not felt in years – peace.

"Test Him. See if He is not true to His word. Cast your bread upon the waters of faith and see if it does not return to you a hundred fold. Trust Him!"

The Pastor emphasized his words with fists punching the air, and the Spirit made sure the message landed on receptive hearts.

The mother of two sat in her church pew and thought about the strange language the pastor had used. Casting bread upon water was a strange notion to her. She visualized what it was like as a child herself on the beach with her parents. She could still hear the sea gulls and the noise of the blue ocean waves and frothy white caps as they rushed to the shore to tickle her toes, and then hurried back to where they had been. It was a safe place for her to be – on that distant shore in the safety of her mind. "If I throw bread out onto the waves of course it will come back to shore, but a hundred times as much as what I throw?" It was a puzzle to her. "Just exactly what do I have to lose? Is it possible for my life to be a hundred times better than what it is right now? I'd welcome that for sure", she confessed to herself.

So, this new stranger to Church and visitor in the parsonage came forward with her children in tow from her back pew to the foot of the platform where The Pastor had preached his message, no longer outcasts from the community, God, or the congregation. They were all three immersed in the waters of faith that day and the mother gave to God the only two things of value she had in her fragile world – her two children. And her life didn't just improve for days or weeks or months but rather for several years.

The horrible demons of their past appeared to be gone – until they weren't. But all those demons of their past came back with a vengeance on the night that Amanda found herself tied to a flimsy kitchen chair taken from the parsonage by her father. She was left to dangle on the chair from the bridge railing over the peaceful rolling waters of the Wildcat Creek, tied and left there by her drunken father. She had time to think while she swayed in the wind by a rope across from the abandoned Malfalfa Park where demons were thought to dwell – and rightly so. That was the night when she determined to fight.

The Charles Deam Forest was where Jamie went to escape the realities of a world that had contained elements of madness for him. The forest was where Jamie went to bury the old and diseased bones of that madness. The forest was where he went to find new life.

Late in the fall of Jamie's last year at I.U, he sought refuge in his old friend, the forest. The changing colors that could only be found in southern Indiana's Monroe Morgan and /brown Counties this time of year offered once again the comfort he so desperately sought. Heavy dew, collecting on the waxy leaves of the Sycamore trees, dropped to the ground with a small and quiet thud that could only be heard in such solitude that could be found in such places. Ground mists swirled in front of the lone hiker but grudgingly parted at his passing, only to coalesce again at his departure. A distant crow seemingly laughed at something it found to be amusing, and a single owl asked in return, "at 'whooom' are you laughing?"

Peace. The forest afforded him what his soul required. Sweet, healing, peace.

Jamie arrived at camp site sixteen and dropped his pack on a weathered wooden picnic table. He removed a small but efficient camp spade and dug a shallow grave for the solitary oak leaf he had picked up along the trail. It was a ceremony he had repeated a dozen times on those weekends as a student, but with the final year of school under way at the university, it was necessary to bury the last remains of his earthly father and all the poison he had left behind. Jamie looked up, beyond the canopy of the darkened green boughs of the cedar trees, where his true Father lived, and prayed to God over the leaf. He transferred all the remaining memories of past hurts done to him and his sister and mother into the leaf. He then laid the leaf into its final resting place with no marker of any kind so it could never be found again, covered it, and walked away, leaving the leaf, and his earthly father forever behind. He did not look back.

The day passed and was measured by one incremental footfall after another and with the passing of motion the memories that had plagued the little boy with the angry balled – up fists of rage faded away and at the end of the day had melded into the mists of the forest never to be recognized again. Ghosts. The forest had become a haunt of old and ugly ghosts, so the boy never returned.

It was still several miles back to the fire stand where Jamie had parked his faithful Jeep, so he decided to spend the night on the banks of Lake Monroe suspended between two trees in his red – white – and blue hammock. The day had turned warm which drained him of what energy had remained to him after his emotional exercise at camp site sixteen. His fatigued body, cocooned in the hammock, gently rocked in a gentle night breeze that drove small waves to the shoreline. The odor of fish and water - life that could be found in the lake wafted ashore and blended with the smell of smoke that snaked through the trees from a small campfire where Jamie had cooked his small evening dinner. Off in the distance, some love sick couple had parked their car on the shoulder of the causeway that passed over the lake. The sound from their car radio could be heard in the darkness as it played a familiar tune which had campus history attached to it – '*Stardust*'.

Jamie was familiar with the story of how the song came to be. It had become local folklore how Hoagy Carmichael had sat down on the '*spooning wall*' near the entrance to the I.U. campus. Hoagy supposedly looked up into the star laced sky on a velvet backdrop and as his college memories flooded over him, so too did the melody of what came to be one of the nation's most memorable romantic songs. Jamie was familiar with the lyrics as well, and they troubled him – lyrics about love and he wondered if he should ever take the chance. "What if I am my father's son?"

Jamie rolled onto his side and gazed back into the inky darkness of the forest beyond the dull red light of his modest camp fire as it flickered against the bark of nearby trees and pondered how an old oak tree could drop a seedling and when it came forth - it was an elm or a beautiful mulberry in full bloom. "That's how it is in God's forest", he thought to himself. "The forest of human souls aren't subject to ordinary rules – God can make me into something quite different than my father. God can make me after His own image…not dad's." It was a beautiful thought to Jamie, and it gave him comfort. In that comfort he slept and the hurts and damage from darker evil days washed from him like the grime of a long forgotten day.

The aromatic smells of rotisserie hot dogs and hot buttered popcorn from street vendors permeated the air as little kids walked up and down the sidewalk with paper cones of cotton candy while the marching band played. The girls in the band sported tall white hats with patten leather brims and marched with perfect posture. The boys donned their fancy stretch pants with gold epaulettes on their shoulders. They beat on their drums, swayed from side to side with their flutes and blew on their trumpets. The children watched as the trombone players pushed their slides in and out making the most beautiful music. A colorful clown walked on stilts, towering high above the masses. He wore multi – colored baggy trousers and a red painted smile, and constantly threw out handfuls of confetti from a bag that hung from his side that never ran empty.

Maybe it was because the colorful clown stood so tall above everyone else or perhaps he just saw something that caught his eye off in the distance of his peripheral vision, but the marching band of time stopped at the distraction and time stood still, and all the people stared. It was for just a moment, but a moment was all that was required. The clown walked over to where two children stood. Just mere children in the eyes of time, and the people watched him go.

Jamie and Amanda stood outside the *'Sample Gates'* that allowed entrance to the campus proper of Indiana University – Jamie's alma mater. The clown was puzzled at the emotion of the boy at seeing those gates, but the girl was the biggest puzzle of all. The clown cocked his head and drank deeply the essence of being which permeated the girl. The dark green Army jacket that was covered with medals of heroism was of interest, it was so different from the clothes the clown wore. But there was more about her than what could be seen, he could sense it. And as the boy and girl walked through those gates of higher learning the clown understood. He learned what he was looking for by observing the odd gate as the girl walked not on her own two legs but on those made of metal. The girl had given part of herself in a warriors fight against evil, and the clown was touched by what he saw.

And as time stood still, the clown walked ahead of the boy and girl. He reached deep in his bag and ceremoniously laid red, white, and blue confetti ahead of the girl. The clown did not look back at the two children but rather returned to the marching band and the procession of time. The music began once again in earnest and the marching band proceeded to a point ahead – just over the horizon where even time would be no more. And all the people laughed, and clapped, and followed.

Jamie and Amanda walked through and past the *'Sample Gates'* a short distance and stood on a raised sidewalk looking at a game of pick up football in *'Dunn Meadow'*. It was an open field lined on one side by maple trees, sycamores, and oaks. A creek that went by the name *'The Jordan River'* passed under a stone arched bridge where a student stood looking at the game but became distracted by the figures of Jamie and Amanda on the distant sidewalk. The lone figure pointed at them and shouted something at the kids playing football and the game and noise stopped.

The stone bridge was draped with the patriotic red, white, and blue of the American flag and Amanda noticed that the sidewalk which surrounded the field flew the American flag as well. The student on the bridge placed his hand over his heart and faced the warrior girl. Every young man and woman on *'Dunn Meadow'* stood in silence and paid homage to Amanda and she was deeply touched.

Amanda had been invited to the campus that day in May to be the keynote graduation speaker at Assembly Hall. She would tell them about sacrifice and duty. Some of that graduating class would be called upon to pay that ultimate price. A payment made in order to stamp out evil and ignorance and darkness, just as she had. And she would remind them of something The Pastor of Howard County had once learned from his own father and spoke of it from the pulpit often:

"Everything in life comes with a price son, nothing in life is free. There is a price to be paid for doing nothing and there is a price that you will have to pay for getting involved. Everything exacts a price. Also, if you choose to get involved, there will be a

payday someday. But, just like the thirty pieces of silver, you may not always like the payment..."

The loss of her leg was a price she had been willing to pay in order to do what she could to stamp out evil – at least as much of it as she could. Evil appeared to her to be able to give birth to other evil children. Stomp on one and another seemed to pop up; like one giant game of *'Whack a Mole'*, it just never stopped. Amanda gave herself consolation that at least she never suffered betrayal like Jesus had.

Amanda did something else that fine day in May. She did what warriors do. She went the extra mile and offered something to the graduating class which the college of higher learning could not. She would impart spiritual truth. Amanda would conclude her own thoughts by reading a poem that she had written while lying in a bed in the surgical ward of a military hospital. Warriors are afforded time for such things while awaiting titanium legs.

A Warrior's Prayer

There is a River Jordan
That all must cross in time.
When with the mighty hand of God
He parts that river dry
So we may cross to golden sands
On shores where mortals die.

His lighthouse stands a distance yet for me
But I can see its beam.
It calls me to a place of rest
Where evil men won't be.

A battle still this seems to be
The warriors struggle against all odds
Through trumpet blast or death's last cry
What price to pay to be up there
With Jesus to abide.

Twas sin that held Him there
Suspended twix earth & sky
So I could visit with the King
To live & never die.

Chapter Nine

THE WATCHMAN – "A STORM IS COMING"

Amiel walked the ramparts of Earth alone. His brothers in arms were gone – fallen like the earth below. His brethren had deserted their ancient posts and divine appointment and abandoned him there as well. They were not content with their assignments to watch and protect – they wanted what they saw for themselves. They were entitled – they were the watchers; the angels of old. They were discontent to watch so in rebellion they subverted the will of God and driven by pride and disobedience they enslaved His creation. Lucifer drove the humans to an appointment with death and so used death as his leasehold to what he so desperately sought – dominion over earth and man. So Amiel walked alone and watched alone but one angel is enough.

He walked the walls on the day the woman fell to the crafty deceptions of the devil. He watched as only one man and his family escaped the floodwaters of a sin filled earth, and when the immorality of Sodom and Gomorrah was burned alive. And again just one man and his family were spared. Amiel – his name means 'God of my people'. God has always had a people. So Amiel walked the ramparts of Earth alone. But he became distracted by the presence of another man. That's the way it always is – the presence of just one righteous man is called upon to make the difference. He studied the life of someone who was called 'The Pastor of Howard County' and determined to point out his presence to the Father because God has always had a people, even if it is just one man. Yes, Amiel would visit This Pastor of Howard County.

> *"No one knows about that day or hour, not even the angels in heaven, nor the Son, but only the Father. As it was in the days of Noah, so it will be at the coming of the Son of Man. For in the days before the flood, people were eating and drinking, marrying, and giving in marriage, up to the day Noah entered the ark: and they knew nothing about what would happen until the flood came and took them all away. That is how it will be at the coming of the Son of Man..." (Matthew 24: 36 – 39)* NIV

There wasn't anything out of the ordinary in his life that should have triggered such a dream for The Pastor. It was a life altering, personality transforming, gut wrenching dream – the kind that comes from another place than the human subconscious mind. If someone were to ask him, and if he were inclined to speak of the dream, The Pastor would say that the dream came from God.

The baseball team he was coaching as a volunteer that Summer in his off hours was having an incredible winning season. Counseling sessions at the Church were mostly young couples with an axe to grind involving household chores and who contributed the most to the marriage, and how they felt overlooked and neglected. They were good kids really who merely needed to be reminded of how much they had been given in life; and how much they had to lose. Usually what they had most to lose had names of children.

The Pastor had seen so much change in his life, and life after the dream would change more than at any other time.

His close friend and Elder, Wayne, was gone. The old farmer just could not win his battle against an aging and failing heart. Also, several months had passed since the final occupant of the little white parsonage behind the brick Church of Christ at the far end of Main Street had left. Sunday School classes now took turns using the abandoned space for lessons and small group gatherings. Diver Dan looked a bit lost sitting on his perch atop the hand carved mantle that was left behind by Theo so many years before. His blue eyes continually searched for someone familiar but seemingly never really found who he was looking for.

Perhaps the evening news had spoken to his spirit and had found its way into his dream, giving him premonitions of ominous times ahead. Or maybe it was the gross immorality and openly flagrant disregard for Biblical marriage on television and other media. But one thing was certain, The Pastor could see in his mind's eye, a plain white door with five tiny little fingerprints. Someone had opened a door that was intended to remain shut. It opened into Huxley's *Brave New World* where societal thinking is an engineered process designed to align with a supposedly progressive culture. Pandora waited behind that door and the door would not shut. And so God Himself warned The Pastor about what was about to come – on the other side of that door.

What had begun as a beautiful Saturday with pleasant, sunny skies and energetic people mowing their lawns and planting colorful flowers of red, yellow, and blue turned into something quite different. The blue jay that kept residence in the birdhouse outside the pastors office window had gone into hiding. The once pleasant afternoon now had a disquiet in the air. He had been scheduled to coach an afternoon baseball game that Summer day, but it was called off due to the ominous weather forecast in Hoosier land. So, instead, he utilized his time to finish his sermon for the morrow in the privacy of his office at his home.

No one would bother him in the private confines of his home office/study. No one would pop their head in the door to say hello like they would have had he chosen to study at the Church. He sat in the quiet of his own space and reflected upon life as he so often did. A preacher of The Word did that sort of thing – think about life - and this pastor more than most perhaps.

He swiveled his chair so he could look out the window and watched as the sky quickly turned dark - punctuated by a brilliant arc of lightning as it raced from the east to the west and was gone, only to be replaced by another burst of light. The thunder seemed directly over The Pastor's house and shook his office. "A storm is coming," he thought to himself. Indeed: a rather sizable storm was coming.

It seemed so long ago to The Pastor of Howard County when he had sat in that same office and waited for Wayne to arrive and discuss purchasing the little white house on Wickersham for the homeless. So much had changed. They did indeed purchase the little house behind the church, and multiple people had used it as a transition between adversity and hope. "The parsonage" sat empty, now however, and a chamber of The Pastor's heart felt empty also as he thought back over the course of events in his life.

He pondered over the Garden of Eden and just exactly what would have motivated a mighty fallen angel to become such a thorn in the flesh to anyone and everyone. The Pastor reflected over the Apostle Peter's words that *"with the Lord a day is like a thousand years, and a thousand years are like a day."* "I wonder if time is something unique to humankind. I wonder if the creation of everything we know which took only six days to a human, had been an expansive amount of chronology in the spirit realm?" "Was our little blue marble on a black velvet backdrop the motivator behind war in the heavens? Or perhaps God's handiwork in the world of Eden became their temptation?" The pastor sat and brooded over truths and speculations; questions that seemingly had no answers. He wondered just exactly how and why things turned out as they did, and what would happen to the future of mankind if the portents which were so consistently conveyed in the evening news were not altered.

A rather powerful jolt of thunder clapped directly over the pastors desk and sent the shiny silver balls of his Newton's Cradle rocking back and forth. As the preacher sat, in the darkness of the storm, and gazed on the movement of the cradle he became drowsy. And as the rain began to fall in a steady drum beat the man's eyes became heavy and sleep took him away.

It was then that the dream came and the plain white door that should have remained shut was fully opened, and The Pastor's life would be forever changed.

It was a strange and unknown sensation that fell upon The Pastor that afternoon. He was quietly sleeping in his office chair, but he could still see everything in the room just as before - but as if it were dimly lit. He watched as the Newton's cradle softly clanged in cadence with the beating of the rainfall from the summer storm. He could still see out of his window, even in his sleep, and saw the lightening play across the darkened sky – only as looking through the thick glass of slumber and puzzled on how this can be.

As he attempted to make sense of his situation, something began to materialize in front of him. It was like sparklers from the Fourth of July celebration at first. Then the air began to take on movement and form when the sparklers clung to the form of what appeared to be a body. And then that body spoke:

"My name is Amiel, I walk the ramparts of Earth. I am the messenger who has been sent to tell you – listen to the dream, it is a message from the Father." And as the frightened dreamer tried to make sense of his situation, he could hear the words of the angel of God repeat his command as his voice drifted off into a distant place; a place where the watcher walked the ramparts. *"Listen to the dream."*

Two massive sandaled feet stood before The Pastor. The tanned feet were as large and as tall as any man - made building. The meticulously woven brown leather that made up each sandal was not new but rather well-worn from years of wear and diligent work. As he looked upon the humble sandals a giant hand reached down and picked him up and tenderly sat the preacher on the lap of one whose garment was made of fine white linen and wrapped in a sash of gold with crimson red fringe and tassels. He saw no face – it was not allowed.

A royal blue story book of sorts, covered with mysterious and rich gold lettering which was unfamiliar to humans appeared out of thin air. The giant allowed the tiny pastor to sit in his lap like a much loved and dear child being read a bed – time story from a priceless and rare old book. But the book was not an ordinary story book – it was alive. Within its sacred bindings was where time itself lived, along with every deed ever done and every thought ever conceived of by humankind. Time was set there within the limits of the front and back covers of the precious book. But when the book was opened, it's awful truth was revealed. But more importantly for The Pastor, the little white door existed there, too, opened to him, and it was never to be closed again. The Pastor saw life and time and the human experiment - through the Father's eyes, and what he saw in his dream that after-noon broke his heart.

The Pastor of Howard County heard in his dream the soft creaking of the leather spine of the old tome and wasn't just able to see the events contained in the pages of life, but he was transported mentally and shown what the book wanted him to witness. The book conveyed not only knowledge but also powerful emotions. His mind was in limitless space but in all its darkness that space was punctuated with the bright lights of other planets and stars and had order and movement. He was told of a dimension which had been completely and utterly void, but God had used it as an artist's canvas on which to paint. God did not merely paint with color but also with love, patience, kindness, and gentleness. The adoration of a benevolent maker permeated everything the pastor could see and sense. The most amazing thing to behold however was the globe of blue, white and brightness. The earth was alive with color and emotion. It stood out from all of God's creation and The Pastor could sense and feel what God the creator had felt – satisfaction, joy and pride. Pride in a job well done. The earth was the crowning jewel of a magnificent masterpiece which was made simply from the mind of its creator. But there were others who looked upon the great masterpiece and wanted it for themselves. They wanted the world of Eden.

Another page was turned, and The Pastor witnessed a familiar scene – he had been there before. He had seen the 'Tree of Life' within the Garden of Eden with its scarlet red bark. Traces of pure silver tracing through it from core to core, like the silver blood of extreme royalty. Its canopy of silver leaves with veins of red was an awesome sight and the pride of its creator emanated from it.

He knew that nearby would be 'The Tree of the Knowledge of Good and Evil' with its black trunk and shiny black leaves. But there was something there within that tree which he had not seen in his previous vision. There was an evil presence coiled there within the limbs of the forbidden tree. The book allowed him to not only sense the enemy but to smell him as well. It was the odor of decay and pestilence, plague and death. The presence emanating from the serpent was the embodiment of revulsion.

A deep sense of sadness and reality set in as he looked upon the terrible tree, and he realized that the same black tree was alive and well deep within his own heart and soul. The same battle that Adam and Eve had faced and failed at was the very battle that he himself faced and fought daily – the battle of good and evil. He, like every other human ever given breath, faced the same temptation to eat of the bad fruit of the Tree of the Knowledge of Good and Evil. "How often have I eaten of its fruit myself – daily? Multiple times daily?" The pastor contemplated the epic battle for the enslavement of the human soul by sin, rebellion against one's own creator, and corruption. "If not for the work of God's own Son, I would be an outcast as well – and rightly so." He was overcome with the conviction of who he was without the presence of God's Holy Spirit and the forgiveness of The Father.

He did not hear the conversation between the serpent of darkness and the rebellious daughter of God. Nor did he witness the heartbreaking fall of humankind that dreadful day. Instead, the pastor was shown the Father's love for an errant creation. He listened as God told Adam and Eve of their punishment for disobedience and betrayal. But the book conveyed something else as well; the determination of God to set things aright. God Himself would pay the price for man's unfaithfulness and the air of the book hung with the weight of that moment in time. It was the moment when sin was eternally judged and so too the eventual ruin of the fallen angels who had provoked such an awful thing.

The pastor watched as Adam and Eve clung to one another and left their home behind. They had never cried before. I t was a new and unwelcome sensation to them. Their tears would not stop however until the day they did indeed die.

The book's attention then turned to the beautiful garden – abandoned and empty – and The Pastor sensed heartbreak coming from a loving Father and His sense of betrayal by his earthly creation and the ones He had once called friends of God in His own realm of heaven. The two trees were uprooted and removed from the world of men and the garden of God took on the form of fallen earth with weeds, thorns, and thistles. A pool of blood was there in the garden where an animal had been slaughtered in order to provide the departing couple their initial covering: an animal that Adam perhaps had given a personal name. The air was filled with the sense of loss and the broken heart of God, and The Pastor cried. -- And the page was turned.

The Pastor had worked many colorful jobs during his lifetime, to put it mildly. He remembered with particular distaste the summer he was hired by a local mortgage company to clean out old, abandoned houses. People who were evicted for any number of reasons, tended to be angry, and left the most awful messes imaginable behind for someone else to clean up. The Pastor had been that 'someone else'. The stench in those homes was horrendous. Spoiled food sat in refrigerators for months or more covered in mold and green slime. Untended pet messes sat in the middle of floors. Soiled furniture was left behind, and dirty diapers were piled up in corners like a city dump. Those homes sat for months or even years in the summer heat with no electricity which cooked the refuse into a stew of putrefaction. Flies, gnats, rodents and cockroaches loved what was left behind, and they were always there to meet the cleanup man when The Pastor first opened the door. -- "If the righteousness of man is as filthy rags to the Father in heaven," he pondered, "then this is what unbridled and rampant sin must smell like," he thought to himself as he looked at a new page. The blue story book covered with rich gold and ancient lettering, conveyed the disgusting truth of sin. He crinkled his nose as the distasteful odor wafted off the people who lived on planet earth during the time of Noah. Wave upon wave of foul odor rose from the world of Noah.

In a clearing of cut – down trees stood a solitary massive boat that towered high above the neighboring landscape of an undisturbed and pristine forest that belonged to another age. A preacher of the Word of God had toiled tirelessly, for years, to build the ship of salvation for the animals of God's creation, and a select handful of people. His own little family – the only survivors of a sin ravaged world - and the creatures; waited for the ark of God which Noah had built to leave an unredeemable earth behind.

News of the spectacle of the giant boat traveled far and wide which drew spectators from the distant reaches of the realm to see the wooden hulk that was propped upright by thick and mighty timbers because there was no sea. The crowds did not throw sticks or stones because they were content to hurl insults at the man of God and his tiny family, but the preacher would not be dissuaded from his calling until his task was complete.

And there it was again - the unmistakable rending of the heart of God for a world of rebellious people who did not know right from wrong and could not see the difference. Theirs was a culture that was built upon the crumbling foundation of self. Darkness to them had become light. The direction of up had turned down. They practiced every form of licentiousness that their evil hearts could imagine and condemned those who said they were wrong to do so. It was the judging of others that became the wrong. Violence claimed the land.

So the heart of God was once again broken as rivers of tears flowed from the face of a benevolent maker whose handiwork had once again betrayed Him. His tears fell in torrents and lifted the ark of God and filled the earth. The Pastor sat on the giant's lap and squinted to see the ship of salvation plowing through the waters of sin. He "strained to see through the wind - driven rain, but it was no use; the ark of God which Noah had built was gone." **(The Majik Carpet Rides of Betty & Billy: Xulon Press, 2020, p.173)** Above the din of the storm he could hear the choked voice of God, asking, "what else could I have done? What would you have done pastor? What would you have done?" – And another page was turned.

To the naked eye they were but two cities – nothing out of the ordinary that would have alerted a casual observer to be alarmed or wary. But the blue story book of a holy and righteous God conveyed the true spirit of the people living there and the evil that could be found there. Mothers taught their daughters and fathers instructed their sons in the ways of wickedness, and their society in turn taught them all – and the devil laughed heartily at what he had been able to do there. He molded them all into deformed beings of once - men who did the bidding of the deceiver of humans. Demons were free to walk the city streets of Sodom and Gomorrah in a dimension that overlayed the reality of those citizens who 'pride'fully called that place home.

The Pastor studied the two cities and mulled over in his mind just exactly how his own culture was traveling down the same broken pathways of an old and failed attempt to live worse than animals. Schools taught children that there was no difference between a boy and a girl. High courts handed down rulings that resulted in the unborn being thrown away like common trash. Super - heroes of the past took on the form of perversity in comic books giving their approval for modern youth to do the same. People flew the multi – colored flag of the rainbow and took pride in who they were and what they had become. The Pastor knew all the while that neither story, the one he was watching, nor the one he was living, would end well.

As a young er man, Lot and his uncle had accumulated so much wealth between them, the land could not sustain them both. Lot was being told – not asked – told, to leave it all and escape with nothing but the shirt on his back, leaving all his worldly possessions behind. Everything that Lot had felt to be of any importance or worth was to be burned as if it had no value at all. "I suppose that is how it will be with us as well." The Pastor reasoned to himself. *"Come out of her my people, so that you will not share in her sins, so that you will not receive any of her plagues."* (Revelation 18:4b) NIV. The man of God knew the Bible passage quite well, and it seemed to him more relevant now for his lifetime than he had ever thought possible. And the weight of the moment was heavy on him.

A deep sadness fell upon the heart of The Pastor who watched as the tome of God revealed Lot leaving his home, hand in hand with his wife. His daughters fearfully and tentatively trailed close behind. Soon in the story, Lot took nothing with him but the ones he loved, and soon he would not even have that. Lot may not have taken anything with him, but his children did – the evil that was sewn into the fabric of their souls by a corrupt and evil culture. It would not take long for such a soured learning to bear the seed of corruption that would haunt the children of God for generations to come. "It's hard to unlearn," thought the pastor. "We are all the sum total of our life's decisions and learning."

The pastor recalled an article he had read about Alfred Hitchcock. When Hitchcock was asked why he always panned away from the most fearful and intense scenes in his films, the director commented that the human imagination was able to paint a far more frightening mental image than the camera could ever begin to create. That was not the case with the destruction of Sodom and Gomorrah, however. The Pastor saw, in living color, the full wrath of an angry God and it was terrifying. He watched in horror as children caught fire and heard the livestock scream in agony as they aimlessly ran wild while they were being burned alive. The homes, the golden fields of grain, and the town square where Lot had encountered the two messengers of God – all on fire, and the screams of the once - men imprinted its unforgettable horror on the mind of him who sat in the giant's lap.

And Lot's story continued.

The early morning sun was blotted out by acrid black smoke. Intense heat radiated from the cities into the backs of the fleeing refugees. Hot soot landed on their clothes and burned their hair and scalp The previously lush and flourishing valley had been turned into a dying furnace from hell. The wail of terror and the presence of apoc-alyptic destruction were too much for the wife of Lot. She turned and beheld the nightmare that God had tried to spare her from. She gained the knowledge she sought but forfeited her life in the process. She had learned the lesson of Eve that some knowledge is just not worth the price. The price to Lot was the loss of his wife. She had been transformed into a life statue of salt for the wild animals to dissolve one lick at a time. – And the pages turned, and turned, and turned…

A mighty wind swirled and turned the book's pages franticly as if caught up in a powerful cyclone, and time veritably flew by. The breeze from the fluttering pages blew into The Pastors face causing him to squint and swat at his hair so he could see. Decades and centuries passed before his eyes. Nations rose and fell. Peoples arrived and vanished like a vapor and just as quickly as they had appeared they became mere footnotes in history as the divine and eternal purpose and plan of God developed. The pages eventually slowed, and The Pastor could began to recognize familiar sights and sounds. He witnessed the ships of the brave explorer Columbus sailing through uncharted waters and the Mayflower. He observed the first feast of Thanksgiving celebrated in a new land. The ragged but hopeful pilgrims had sailed to a foreign place of refuge, seeking to live in peace and spiritual freedom. Majestic mountains appeared, surrounding rolling hills and valleys of planted corn and wheat. Rivers of crystal blue waters flowed, and fish could be seen swimming as if viewing them through pure glass. And The Paster knew he was observing the birth of purity in a new land whose citizens looked to God rather than kings of old for guidance and direction. There was love between the Creator and those who sought Him, and The Pastor sensed satisfaction and peace between God and man. – but the pages turned...

The horsemen of plague, pestilence, and disease passed before the eyes of The Pastor of Howard County, and he witnessed scenes of what he hoped would not become reality. People lived in fear – fear of the air and fear of others around them. They covered their faces to hide from the things that lurked unseen. Dark midnight skies were turned bright orange from the firelight of burning cars and trucks and buildings. Hostile mobs, filled with extreme anger, hatred, and violence, roamed city streets. Molotov cocktails were thrown at police cars while their lights of red, blue and white Illuminated the skies, and screaming sirens punctuated the air. The story book was showing him his own time. He could smell the exact same putrid odors that had come from the world of Noah and the twin cities of Lot's age. The cycle of sin had brought him back to his own time and like Lot, the place he himself called home.-- And the pastor knew...

The stone arches and ramparts on which Amiel walked, shook and trembled with a terrible violence. He looked up into the heavens and saw a comet as if it were a mighty mountain, ablaze and arcing across the morning sky. Its long tail was filled with smoke, fire and rocky debris as it crossed over the place where the watchman stood. Demons from hell followed in its path. The blazing mountain was headed toward the earth and Amiel knew… ***"A storm is coming, a terrible, terrible storm is coming."***

Chapter Ten

REFLECTIONS

I t was winter – in every way. The editorial writer lay in her bed alone and listened to the raging blizzard outside her Hoosier log home nestled in the privacy of the Brown County woods. She was alone because that's what she wanted. She chose to live a life without the constraints of a relationship or anyone telling her what or who she could be. She ate what she wanted, came and went as she pleased, when she pleased. She needed no one. But, as she tossed and turned, trying to ignore the winter storm, she thought she could hear the wind calling her name in the most forlorn and mournful way. It was just her imagination, and she knew it – at least she hoped so.

The frozen oak tree standing sentry outside her window swayed like a drunken troll casting ominous shadows across the bedroom walls. Its icicle fingers raked against the glass like a child with bare nails on a chalkboard, sending shivers down her back. Sleeping was hopeless, so she traded her warm blankets for a cup of hot tea in the cozy comfort of her open kitchen with the cross - beamed vaulted ceiling.

The solitary journalist sat at the kitchen island looking out on her own space, decorated to her own taste and specifications. She never had felt lonely before but the howling wind was relentless and continued to call out her name as if trying to find her in the darkness. For the first time in her life, she knew what it was like to be all alone. The lights sputtered and arced when the power eventually surrendered to the storm and failed - and then the house went pitch black. So, she moved over to the picture window that looked out upon the wintery tumult until the back – up generator kicked in. A distant security light that still had power illuminated the snow that was blowing sideways like a snow globe that never stopped - shaken by some mighty unseen hands. It seemed to her as if the distant light was the headlamp of a massive loco-motive that was bearing down on her. She felt as though something unseen was heading toward her and she was desperately trying to run away.

Perhaps it was her assignment the next day, to inter-view the mother of The Pastor of Howard County, that drove her thinking. She stood for long moments looking out the window, at nothing particular. She whispered into the dark of the storm: *"Are you real?"* She spoke into the void of the night. The only proof that she had spoken at all was the fog from her breath that obscured her vision through the frosty glass. With a shudder, she reprimanded herself for allowing the walls of her personal resolve, to live by her own rules and standards, to come down even for the briefest of moments. She tried to block out the raging weather and returned to her bed where she tossed and turned until ' *her* ' own personal storm had passed.

The morning sun illuminated the snowy deposit from the previous night's gale, sending glistening bursts of light across the landscape like a beautiful sequin gown. The words that were spoken the night before were conveniently forgotten by the journalist – safely delegated to a place where they could not resurface – or so she thought. The spoken word did not mean so much to her – she was a writer. It was the written word that mattered in her world. What was communicated verbally could be forgotten, but the printed word had a life of its own that time had no effect upon. Yes, it was the written word that she had value for, and she had an appointment to keep. So she did.

It should have been a short drive to Carmel from Little Nashville. Her scheduled appointment to interview the mother of the Pastor of Howard County wasn't until late that afternoon. The snow plows should have had plenty of time to clear the highway, but salt and blades were no match for what the fierce storm had deposited. She plugged the address of her intended destination into her phone's GPS and ventured out warily on the icy roads to Carmel. The drive was treacherous. Her four wheel drive SUV was equipped with mud and snow tires, but they were barely a match for the road conditions. In an act of desperation, the journalist drove off the main road just enough for her passenger tires to ride on the rumble strip of the shoulder hoping for just enough traction to remain on the highway. She would have thanked God for the safe travel as she passed multiple cars in the ditches – if she had believed in God. He was the train that was bearing down on her, like the security light in last night's storm, another appointment she would not miss.

The Pastor's mother's duplex was located on a dead end cul-de-sac in a quaint little part of town. The gas yard light was doing its best to chase away the gray of the sky which attempted to obscure the house sign. The journalist gathered up the tools of her trade and walked up toward the front door of the little bungalow. It was only then she noticed it had begun to snow again – not a blizzard like the previous night but rather a peaceful snow that fell like gentle white feathers. She rang the doorbell, and while she waited to be allowed entry, she took in the presence of the late afternoon – peace. There was a peace in that place which was difficult to find. It seemed to live there, at the home of the mother of The Pastor of Howard County.

The door was opened, and pleasantries were exchanged as the reporter stomped snow from her shoes on the mat just inside the door. Hot coffee was soon placed in her hands by the elderly occupant of the pleasant home. A cross necklace draped around the neck of the old woman, and a devotional rested on an end table next to the chair where the woman apparently spent a great deal of time. Her crossword puzzles, yarn, and some knitting needles were in a basket on the floor. The devotion for that day was 'THE LOST SHEEP'. "Your Father in heaven is

not willing that any of these little ones should be lost."
(Matthew 18: 14). NIV And the woman thought about the
headlamp of the oncoming train and then the wind once
again began calling her name.

Silence hung in the air like a thick fog. The little bird
in the coo- coo clock on the wall across from the woman's comfy chair stuck his head out to see what was going
on - or not going on to be more specific- but decided that
the time of day was the only item of interest to him, so
he retreated back into his little bird house and closed the
door behind him. The journalist sat looking for some elusive thought that hung suspended in her imagination – just
close enough for her to sense it but intangible enough to
avoid being seen. She sat there with her mouth slightly
agape, lost in her thoughts and oblivious to her immediate
surroundings.

"Miss Thomas? Miss Thomas!" the wizened mother
could read the situation without being told. A mother of
a pastor is like that. "*He* is the voice in the darkness who
is calling your name. *He* is the light in the storm. "Miss
Thomas, you don't need to know who you are running
from in order to know who you are running to – but you
must run!"

The real story being written there in the privacy of that
small living area was not new to God. He had written
the story Himself millions of times. It was the story of
redemption, regeneration and survival through salvation.
It was **His story** written on the hearts and minds of human
kind. If the journalist had value for the written word, she

was about to encounter the chisel of God upon the fleshy heart of man.

"How could this total stranger know such a thing?" The writer thought to herself, and her puzzled expression betrayed her secret unspoken feelings. "How could private thoughts and emotions become so obvious and transparent?" She quickly tried to compose herself and sipped the last of her coffee still in her cup.

"Miss Thomas, I don't want to overstep my bounds. I know you are here to do an interview concerning my son, but I'd love for you to evaluate how a life - walk with your true Father makes all the difference in the world. Go ahead and ask me what you came to do and in return, I will ask you to evaluate whether a relationship with God was worth it." And just like the falling down of the walls of Jericho, the walls of resistance did not come down with one pass around her heart but when the walls fell, they would fall all at once and completely, never to be rebuilt again.

With a deep breath and no little amount of will power, Miss Thomas looked around the small room for a point of reference that she could use to draw the woman into an intimate conversation and begin their interview. It was how she was trained. Find something that was an emotional tie to draw someone out. It wasn't very difficult to do within the confines of the old woman's small home. The pastor's mother moved to a couch, beneath an oval wood - framed wedding portrait mounted to the wall behind her. The old woman positioned herself there bravely, as if to protect the memory from intruders who would attempt to steal it away.

"I take it that was your wedding day." The journalist made it a statement of fact rather than a question. It appeared to be obvious. The young red – haired girl with high cheek – bones stood next to a tall, dark haired and handsome young man – boy really – beneath an ivy covered trellis. It was obviously a beautiful, sunny day for an outdoor wedding. The camera assured the new husband he had won the grand prize with the beauty next to him. "Can you tell me a little about that day since that is where the journey began that led to The Pastor of Howard County."

The wizened mother seized the opportunity and used it as her own reference point – a point where she could begin her laps around the walls of Jericho.

"It was my father's last opportunity to take me to worship service while we were all still together as a family. I can only imagine what it must have felt like for him." She gave a nod across the room toward the fireplace mantel where a collage of framed photos stood. In one picture, her daddy stood proudly next to what was then a shiny new Studebaker sedan. "He died when I was just twenty four years old," She said with a quavering voice.

"He was a deacon in the church and all the Elders and Deacons sat together, in what would best be described as a jury box at the front of the congregation facing the pulpit. I sat next to my mother that day and paid attention to the sermon but never let on that I saw my daddy stealing glances at his daughter that day. I suppose it was his own private way of saying good – bye."

The elderly woman then nodded her head toward the portrait in the oval wood frame on the wall behind where she was sitting. "It was a beautiful sunny day – the Sunday I married my Johnnie. We were married in my family's cherry orchard." Her gaze drifted off to another time and place, where only she lived, but never lost track of Miss Thomas. "Can I give you some helpful advice?" She posed the statement as if asking permission to offer something valuable and the journalist nodded her approval to continue. "Never wear white in a cherry orchard!" The suggestion was rendered and accepted with a wink by the elder and a smirk by the writer.

"It was a bittersweet day, Miss Thomas. I had hoped my very best friend, Patsy, would be my maid of honor, but she died of influenza in the hospital while I was to be married. Her sister stood in for her. Poor, poor Patsy. I'll never forget her. A boy from church played the violin and another friend from high school played the accordion. My daddy had my piano brought out of the house and down to the orchard for the wedding."

Precious moments of silence lapsed as the two sat and visualized a day from the woman's past. "What would you trade for a lifetime of memories Miss Thomas? It all comes with a price tag." And somewhere off in the distance, the once – beautiful young redhead could see her Johnnie with his lopsided grin. "I'd pay the price again Miss Thomas. I'd do it all again."

"Do you believe in miracles Miss Thomas? I do." The elder stateswoman plowed ahead and gave no opportunity for her guest to insert doubt into the one – sided conversation. Miss Thomas was no longer conducting the interview at that point. And the elder did not relinquish control of the dialogue.

"My husband and I moved to the Ozarks during our semi – retirement time – out. We left everything behind us, including that old piano of mine. I missed that piano, but it was one of those price tags I was telling you about, Miss Thomas. It wasn't too long after we made the move, when my husband went to bed one night and had a dream. According to my Johnnie, God spoke to him and told him that a local church would call us the next morning and offer to sell me their piano for $75. I got that phone call Miss Thomas, and I bought their grand piano for $75 – a price set by them – not me."

The woman reached out for her cane leaning on the end table near her knitting basket and struggled to her feet. She shuffled gingerly to an organ which sat against the opposite wall and lifted the bench lid to retrieve a small walnut plaque with sheet music decoupaged to it on one side. On the back of that block of wood was the story of the old grand piano bought for $75. "This is what remains of that piano, Miss Thomas," the old woman said as she carefully handed the relic to the young writer. The Pastor of Howard County and one of the Elders of the church had taken that old piano and cut it up into small pieces when the ivory keys would no longer make a sound; when its days were done. "The old piano still plays Miss Thomas. Everyone in the congregation received one of those pieces of her."

Miss Thomas looked at the back of the block of wood and read the story of how God had replaced this old woman's piano so many years prior. She studied the article in her hands and gently turned it over and read the sheet music that told of a rugged cross. She had heard that song before, when she was just a child, and somehow it felt to her as if she was holding a piece – just a small piece – of that old, rugged cross in her trembling hands.

No one heard the cracking sound of foundation stone as it split apart and spewed a chalky white cloud of dust into the air, but the older woman had just completed a lap around the figurative walls of Jericho. The walls that surrounded the heart of Miss Thomas was cracking.

The little coo – coo bird was tied to the small clock and could not flyaway, but time did fly as the mother spoke of a little boy who watched cartoons on Saturday mornings on a television from olden days: a boy that played in the neighborhood tree house and followed his older brother around their boyhood neighborhood like an inseparable shadow sewn together at the hip. The writer took her notes and reminisced with the mother and learned how even the noblest of old men were just naughty little boys at some point in their past.

Miss Thomas was told of a time when the pastor had gone wading in Wildcat Creek wearing his new Sunday shoes and ruined them at a time when money was scarce, and how at the age of four had nearly died on a sucker until his mother had jumped off a loading dock in the town when trying to find someone – anyone who could save the choking little boy. The jolt dislodged the sucker, and the interview dislodged the memory of something traumatic that had happened so long ago. One by one the mother related her stories and Miss Thomas listened with rapt attention and furiously wrote about the somewhat ordinary life of a local legend.

"It sounds like a fun life," the journalist commented. "Oh yes it was, I remember when my mother came for a visit and tripped coming down the stairs. She didn't fall but just a few steps and when I came around the corner, she just sat there and laughed. We both laughed until we couldn't breathe. She liked to come and visit us for Christmas. When asked by one of my sisters why our mother always wanted to visit us for the holidays, my mother simply responded – 'because they know how to laugh'."

She told of the time when the older brother had done something that warranted a spanking and was told to wait until their father got home. The older son had stuffed a pie pan down his little shorts and entered the family kitchen to receive his discipline. "When Johnnie saw what the little rascal had done it tickled his funny bone, and he just dismissed the whole thing, " the mother chuckled at the memory.

"Our kitchen, hallway and dining room made a contin-uous circuit of rooms, and those two boys would chase each other around and around, through those rooms, like a dog chasing its tail. On one of those circuits they knocked over a large potted plant onto my new dining room carpet" "Just keep running the older brother had told the younger." Where to?" he asked. "I don't know but we won't come back until she cools down," his brother hollered back over his shoulder and the two of them ran out of the kitchen, through the garage and into the back yard and kept on running. I didn't see either one of them until the mess was all cleaned up and I had indeed cooled down." The mother rolled her eyes at her mischievous sons and Miss Thomas stopped writing long enough to hold her hand over her mouth which had formed a wide open *'O'*." Oh! those naughty little boys" she said. And the air exploded with contagious laughter.

The mood eventually calmed from frivolity to serious-ness as the writer asked how such a fun loving household was capable of imparting such deep spiritual truth. "Just how did you train your boys along the path of Godliness?" she asked.

"Life is a spiritual journey Miss Thomas; you never stop learning – no matter how old and gray you become. But, as a parent, you need to sow the seeds of prayer, dependence upon our creator, and also a self-reliance on one's own self if one is ever going to be able to help our fellow man – something that is sorely lacking in our current society. I remember a statement I heard a long time ago that we must never become so spiritual minded that we are of no earthly good. God calls us to be both I believe: totally focused upon Him, and also to be a servant to others if we are to truly become good stewards of the time He has allotted to us."

"During the early years of the Church Age there was a man named *'Simon the ecclesiastical pole sitter'*. In an effort to separate himself from the evils of society and focus upon spirituality, he spent his years sitting in complete abstinence from the world while sitting upon the top of a pole. It's awfully hard to help our fallen world while sitting on a pole."

Miss Thomas gave a tentative nod as her mind was directed down a path at the prodding of the mother of the pastor. "Money is always tight in a young family. I recall a time when I should have had a new battery installed in the family car - or had the battery terminals cleaned at the very least. I remember the car stalling out and would not start back up again on U.S. 31. There I was with my two boys, stranded on the shoulder of the highway as cars flew by us. I didn't know a thing about a car's mechanics, and still don't, but it didn't stop me from raising the hood of the car and looking at the engine like I could figure it out. One of the boys popped his head out of the window and asked what they should do. I told them to get in the back seat and pray as I took off one of my high heeled shoes and beat on the battery. When I got back in and turned the key once more, the car started up again. To this day, when I have issues with my car, one of my boys will just say, *'beat on it with your shoe, mom!'*. "To my boys, it was a model of answered prayer."

The journalist could visualize the comical scene as it played out in her mind and chuckled at the sight.

"It isn't enough though, to be wise and spirit minded if we don't know how to put it into motion. I remember getting a phone call from one of the boys while at work. I was instructed to come home immediately and bring one dozen A & W coney dogs and enough root beer for a dozen boys, and then the phone went dead. I played along out of curiosity and did what I was told. When I entered my house there were a dozen boys doing the chores I had instructed my own children to do before they could go outside to play."

"We told them we can't come out and play until the chores are done so I promised them lunch if they would help!" Again, the two women rolled their eyes, but Miss Thomas could see that the patience of the older woman had implanted a sense of personal resilience in her little children.

Another lap had been taken around the heart of the young journalist, which was now beginning to fill up with the wisdom and laughter imparted to her by this wise matriarch, and it tore at the Jericho stones of isolation and indifference concerning the spirit world which she had elected to ignore for far too long. And the vision of Miss Thomas began to change.

The two ladies exchanged stories about life and its difficulties like working through college. The mother told the writer about how her son and husband would work all day and attend Bible College at night. The writer told the mother about her journalism classes and reading C.S. Lewis and how the old woman's front yard made her think about the faun and Mr. Beaver.

The mother told how on each Sunday Edith, with her missing front teeth, would run on stage and jump into The Pastor's lap for the children's mini sermon before going to class. None of the other children dared to take her place. She told about donut Sunday and how the kids passed out candy to the adults before services; it was as sacred to those young souls as if they were tiny little deacons. The journalist was filled with the wonder of a time and place which was filled with such enthusiasm for life and love.

Finally, the interview came to an end. Miss Thomas had used up every cassette tape she had brought in her briefcase for the portable recorder. She packed up her things, thanked the elderly lady with the cross necklace and the touch of red hair among the gray, and turned toward the front door to say farewell. When The Pastor's mother opened the door for her visitor to leave, they both looked out on fresh snow that had fallen during their time together, and the soft glow of the gas light in the front yard. Miss Thomas stood there motionless, taking in the mood of the moment. The afternoon had turned to evening and had come to a conclusion much too soon for her. She had grown attached to the little house and the company she had found there. The pastor's mother knew the heart of her guest and touched her hand ever so softly – just enough to get the attention of Miss Thomas.

"It will be there tomorrow you know," said the old woman. "What will be there tomorrow?" the writer asked. "Work. Work will still be there tomorrow. I have a private guest room and you can leave tomorrow. Won't you please keep me company tonight?"

The offer was accepted with a relieved heart, the door closed, and the night continued. The journalist turned back the blankets to the four- poster bed in the guestroom and opened the blinds to a large picture window across from her bed. She could see the gas light in the front yard as the snow continued to come down. And perhaps it was the mention of reading C.S. Lewis in her college years, but now, in her mind's eye, she could visualize a faun and Mr. Beaver talking while under the yard light. The beaver turned to her and said:

"Miss Thomas, you don't need to know who you are running from in order to know who you are running to – but you must run!" Miss Thomas decided it was indeed time to run, so she ran to the cross.

As she reached down to switch off the lamp beside her bed, she noticed a hand written poem lying on the night stand; undoubtedly written by The Pastor's mother. By the time she finished reading the poem, the walls of Jericho that had surrounded her heart had completely fallen down with a mighty thud, and the earth shook. Only the Savior heard the walls fall down, and He smiled with his own precious smile, and laughed at the joy of another child come home.

Dear Lord Jesus,

My heart is heavy – the day has been long.
I wish I could thank you for everything with a
thankful song.
My voice has weakened, and my body is weak too,
Please lead me for this journey has been
pretty heavy.
I really want to greet you with vigor;
To sing praises and love for all you have done.
What a privilege and joy to serve you with praises.
It's been my desire to please you and see your
smile and hear again the sound of your laughter!

Your faithful servant.

As Miss Thomas lay in her bed, she determined *not* to write the magazine article about 'The Pastor of Howard County' as her editor had assigned. It seemed like too small a thing to dedicate her feeble venture to his noble task. She conspired to tell a much broader tale of the multiple stories lived out during the life of The Pastor. She would use an old, dilapidated parsonage as an avatar to tell his stories of ministry that occupied a life of labor. She imagined wisps of cottonwood being caught up in a summer wind as it flew above tall grasses that swayed in the breeze, an untended front yard given over to seed from years of neglect, and bumblebees as they flew from flower to flower. She would tell the stories of his decades of ministry to an entire county of people. She determined in her heart to write the true stories as told from the viewpoint of the old house at 301 Wickersham.

"I can do it! After all – I'm a writer!" she thought to herself, and drifted off to a place of peace, there in the home of the mother of *'The Pastor of Howard County'*.

CPSIA information can be obtained
at www.ICGtesting.com
Printed in the USA
LVHW081402140322
713408LV00010B/435

9 781662 838583